Table of Contents

How to Use Pop-Up Animals.................................3
Backgrounds..5
Background Patterns.......................................7

Terrier...10

Basset Hound..12

Mutt...14

Cat..16

Bunny...18

Donkey..20

Cow...22

Frog..24

Sheep...26

©1989 by Evan-Moor Corp.

Duck 28

Owl 30

Hen 32

Penguin 34

Bear 36

Reindeer 38

Kangaroo 40

Lion 42

Dragon 44

Rhino 46

Wonderful Ways to Use the Pop-Up Animals

Creative teachers are always looking for unique ways to enhance regular classroom tasks. These pop-up animals can be used in may ways to allow students a chance to become a part of their own learning.

Puppet — Enliven group oral reading time by using pop-up animals as you would use puppets.

Book Reports — Older children can use the pop-up animals as a book-reporting medium. They use the animal to explain how the character felt and acted.

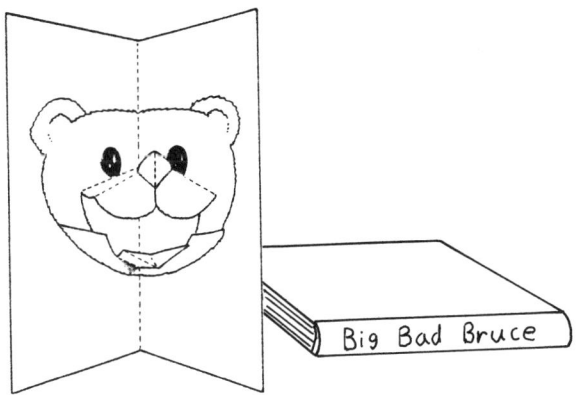

Units — Does the unit or theme that you are working on need another aspect? These animals add that creative touch to what is being studied.

Conversations — Children enjoy being able to talk when they are not exposing themselves. The size of the pop-up makes conversations between two different animals easy at a student's desk.

Creative Writing — When a student is writing for the pop-up animal in a particular situation, the results can be wonderful. Conversation in students' stories can be taught using the animals.

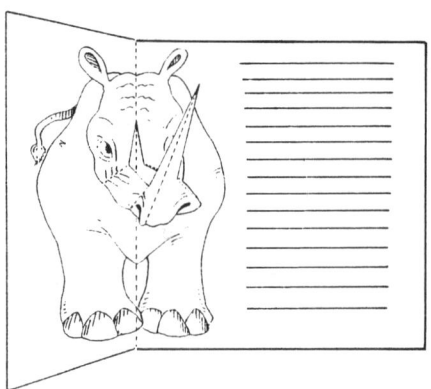

Story Telling — After reading a favorite story to a group of children, the pop-up animals could be used as a bridge to remember a special character or event. This gives another dimension to story telling by letting the students manipulate and create something from the story.

Greeting Cards — One of the pop-up animals plus a special message makes a wonderful greeting card for any special occasion. Everyone, young or old, loves the surprise of opening a card that pops out to greet them.

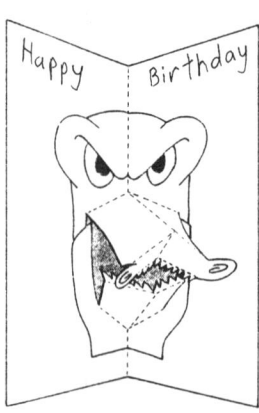

Backgrounds

The background piece for the animals can be a plain piece of construction paper 9" X 12" (22.9 X 30.5 cm) or 12" X 18" (30.5 X 45.7 cm), a sheet of writing paper, a scrap just covering the mouth, or an elaborate setting for the animal.

The backgrounds can be folded in a variety of ways:

1. Horizontally — fold in half.

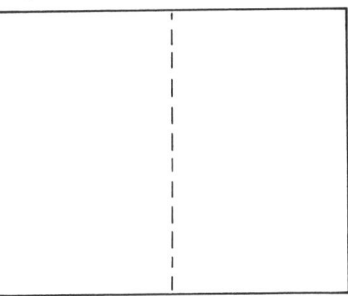

2. Vertically — fold in half.

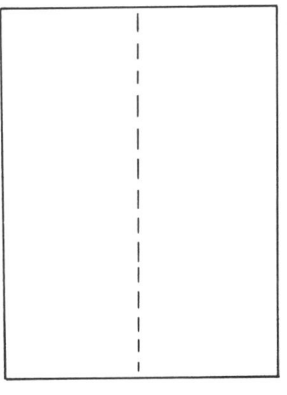

3. Fold just one end — using 12" X 18" (30.5 X 45.7 cm) paper.

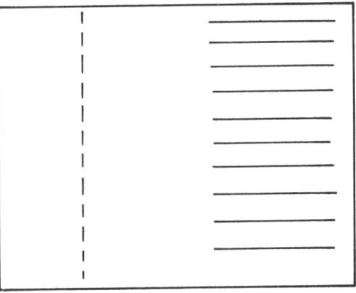

4. Fold both ends — using 12" X 18" (30.5 X 45.7 cm) paper. This fold is perfect for conversations between two characters.

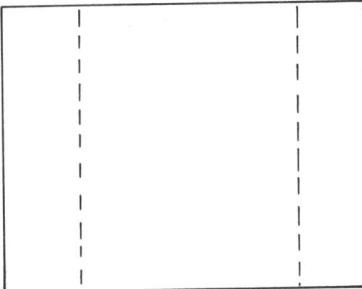

Unusual Backgrounds

Dog in the Doghouse — Use the pattern on page 7 to create a house background. Paste the dog parts to the dog house following the directions given on page 10.

Lion in a Circus Tent — Use the pattern on page 8 to create a circus tent for the lion. Paste the lion parts to the tent following the directions given on page 42.

Penguin — Use the pattern on page 9 to create an icy glacier. Paste the glacier to the background sheet before you paste on the penguin's body and head following the directions on page 34.

©1989 by Evan-Moor Corp.

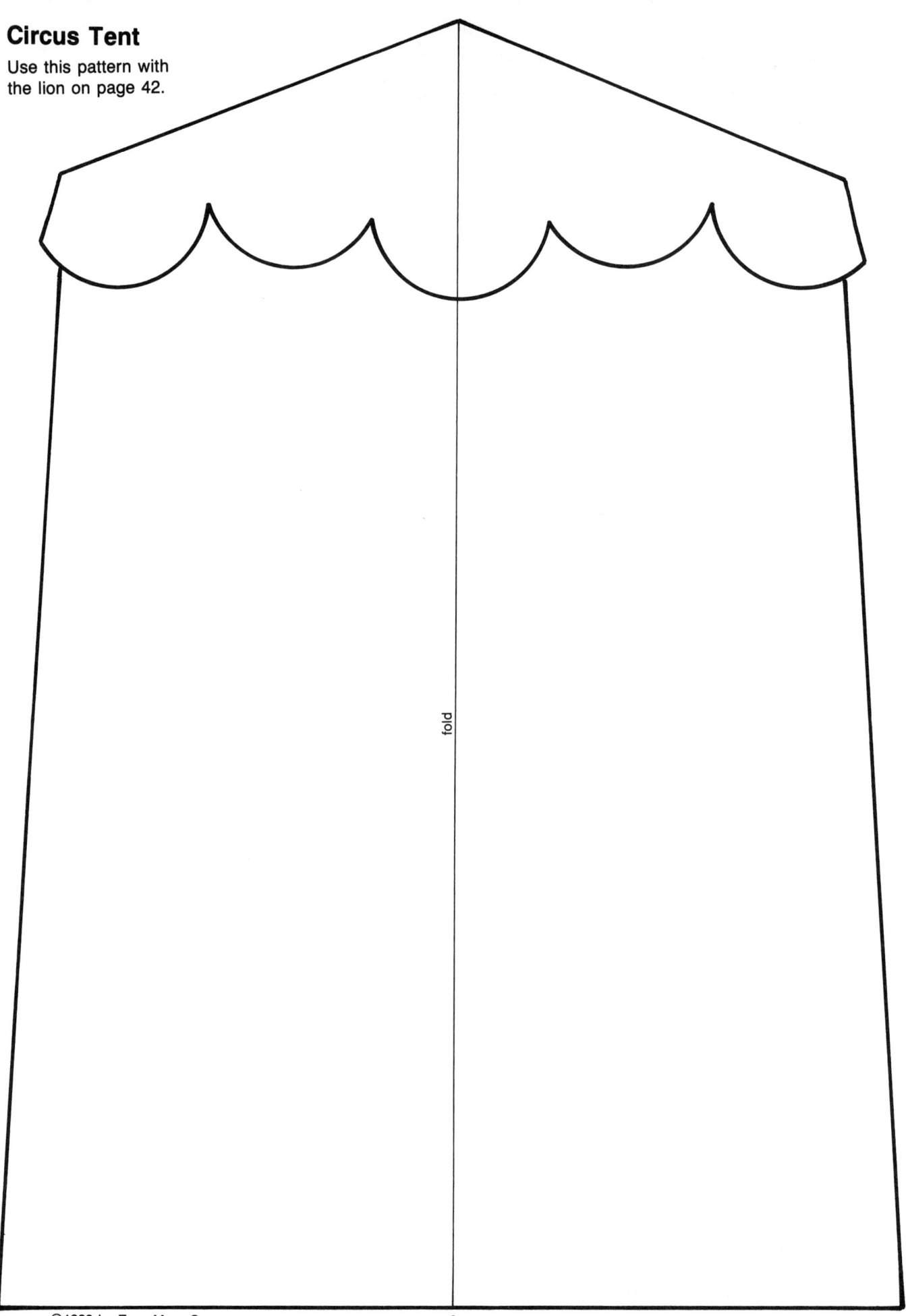

Circus Tent

Use this pattern with the lion on page 42.

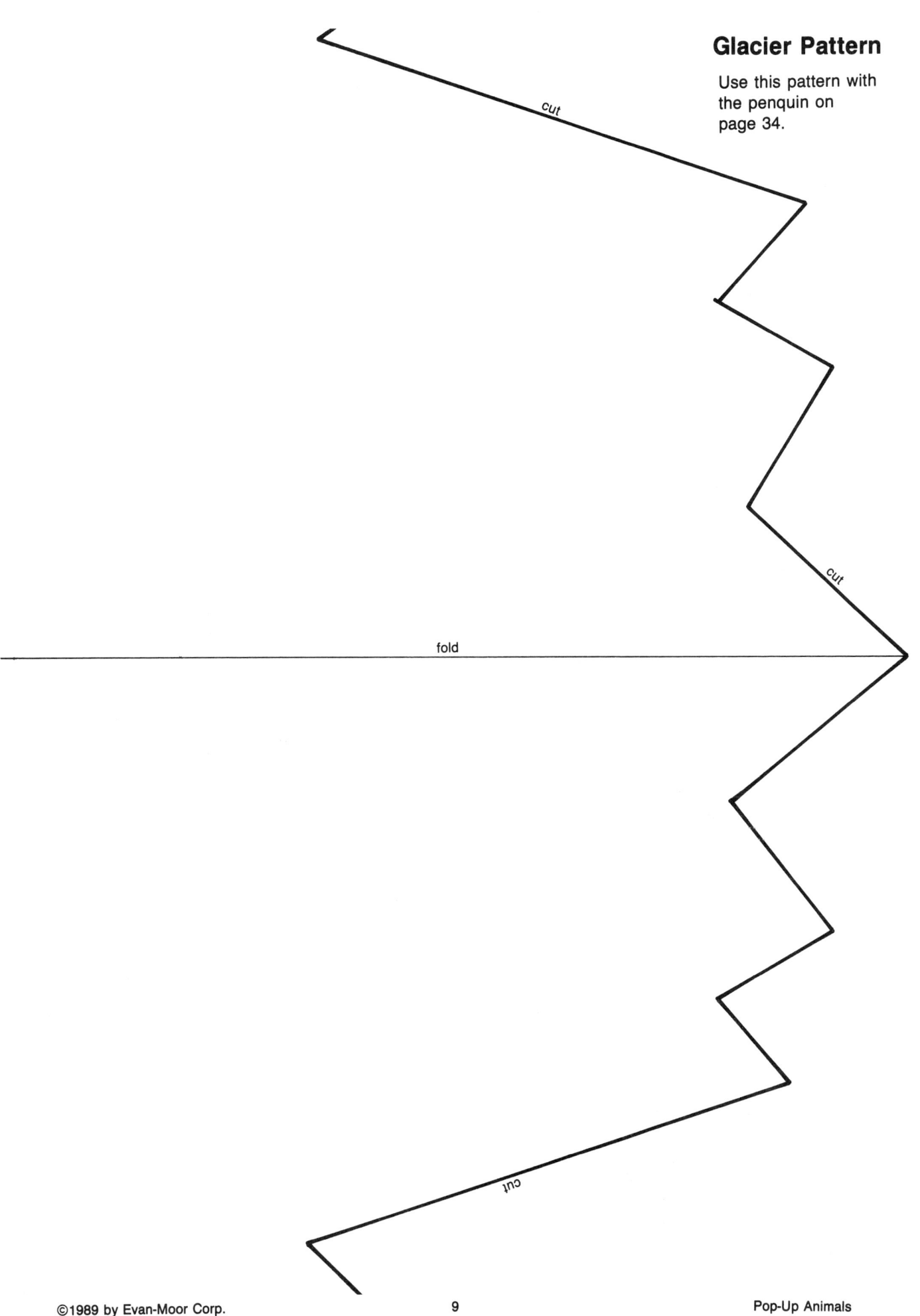

Terrier

1. Color the body parts.
2. Cut on the outside lines.
3. Head:
   a. Fold the head in half on fold 1. The colored side should be on the outside.
   b. Cut the nose line while folded in half.
   c. Fold lines 2 and 3 while folded in half. Fold each line away from you and then again towards you.
   d. Unfold the head. Push the nose up between the ears until the head folds flat.

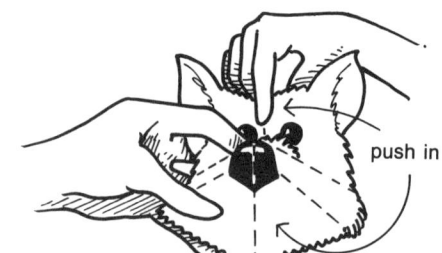

4. Body:
   a. Fold the body in half on fold 1. The colored side should be on the outside.
   b. Make fold 2 while folded in half.
   c. Unfold the body. Reverse the folds and refold to the center. See picture.

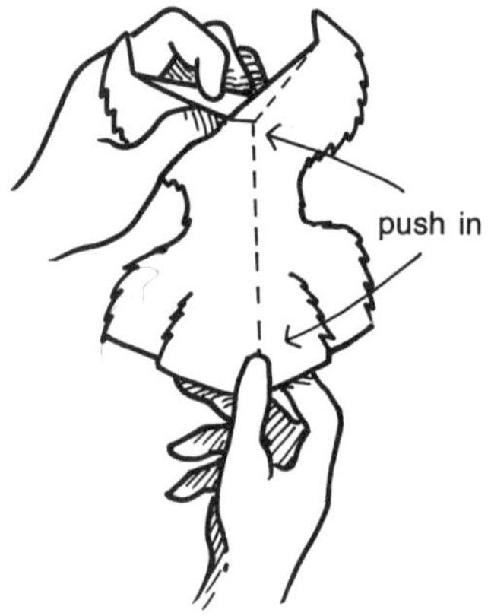

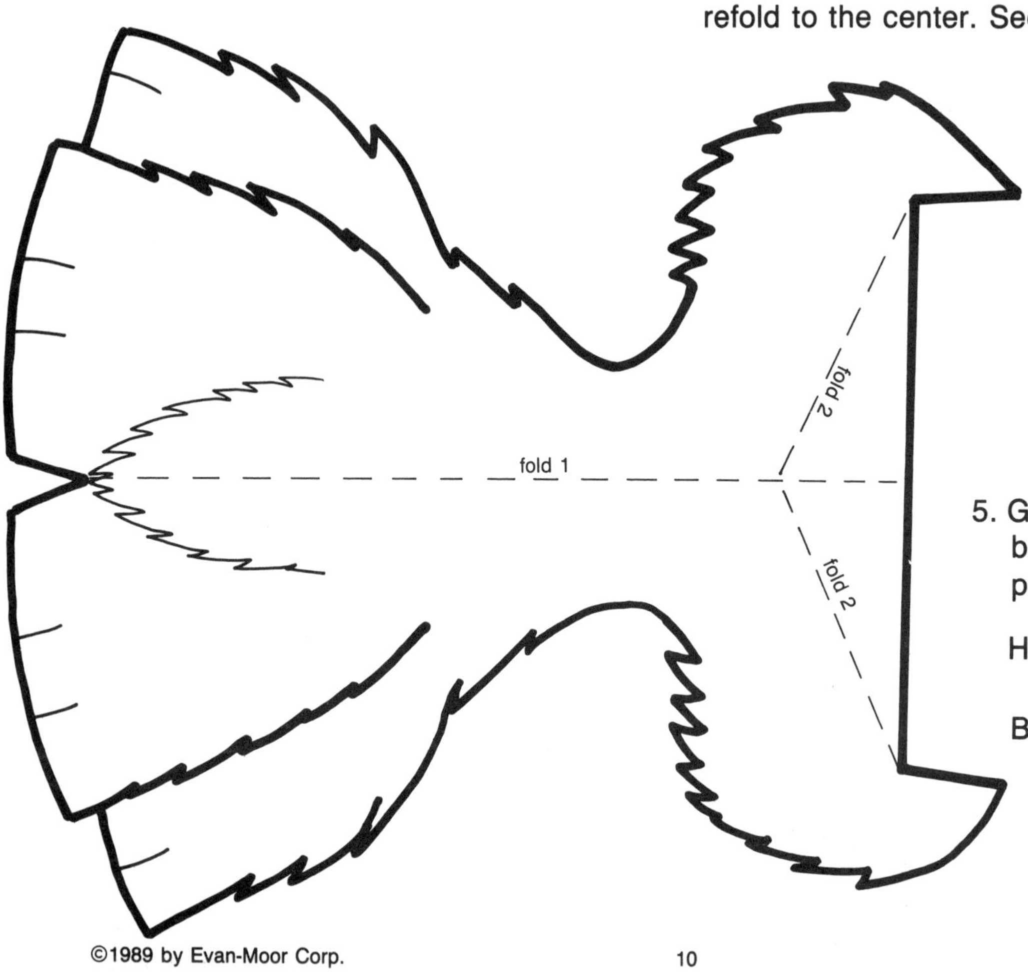

5. Glue the head and body to the background paper.

   Head: Apply glue only above fold 2.

   Body: Apply glue only below fold 2.

©1989 by Evan-Moor Corp.

Pop-Up Animals

Basset Hound

1. Color the body parts.
2. Cut the outside lines.
3. Head:
   a. Fold the head in half on fold 1. The colored side should be on the outside.
   b. Cut the nose line while folded in half.
   c. Fold lines 2 and 3 while folded in half. Fold each line away from you and then again towards you.
   d. Unfold the head. Push the nose up until the head folds flat.

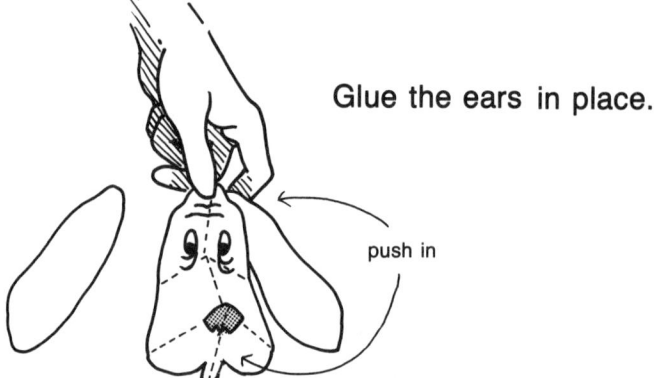

Glue the ears in place.

push in

4. Body:
   a. Fold the body in half on fold 1. The colored side should be on the outside.
   b. Make fold 2 while folded in half.
   c. Unfold the body. Reverse the folds and refold to the center. See picture.

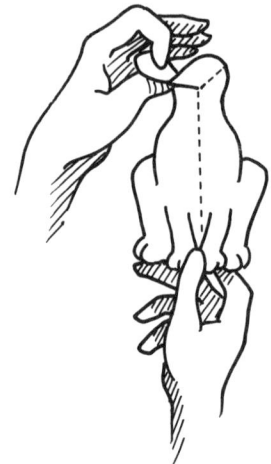

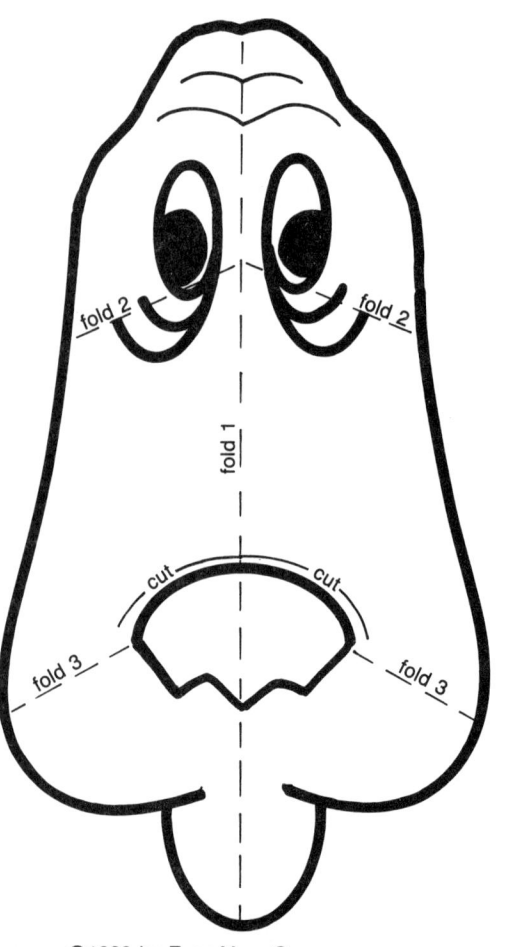

5. Glue the head and body to the background paper.

   Head: Apply glue only above fold 2.

   Body: Apply glue only below fold 2.

©1989 by Evan-Moor Corp.

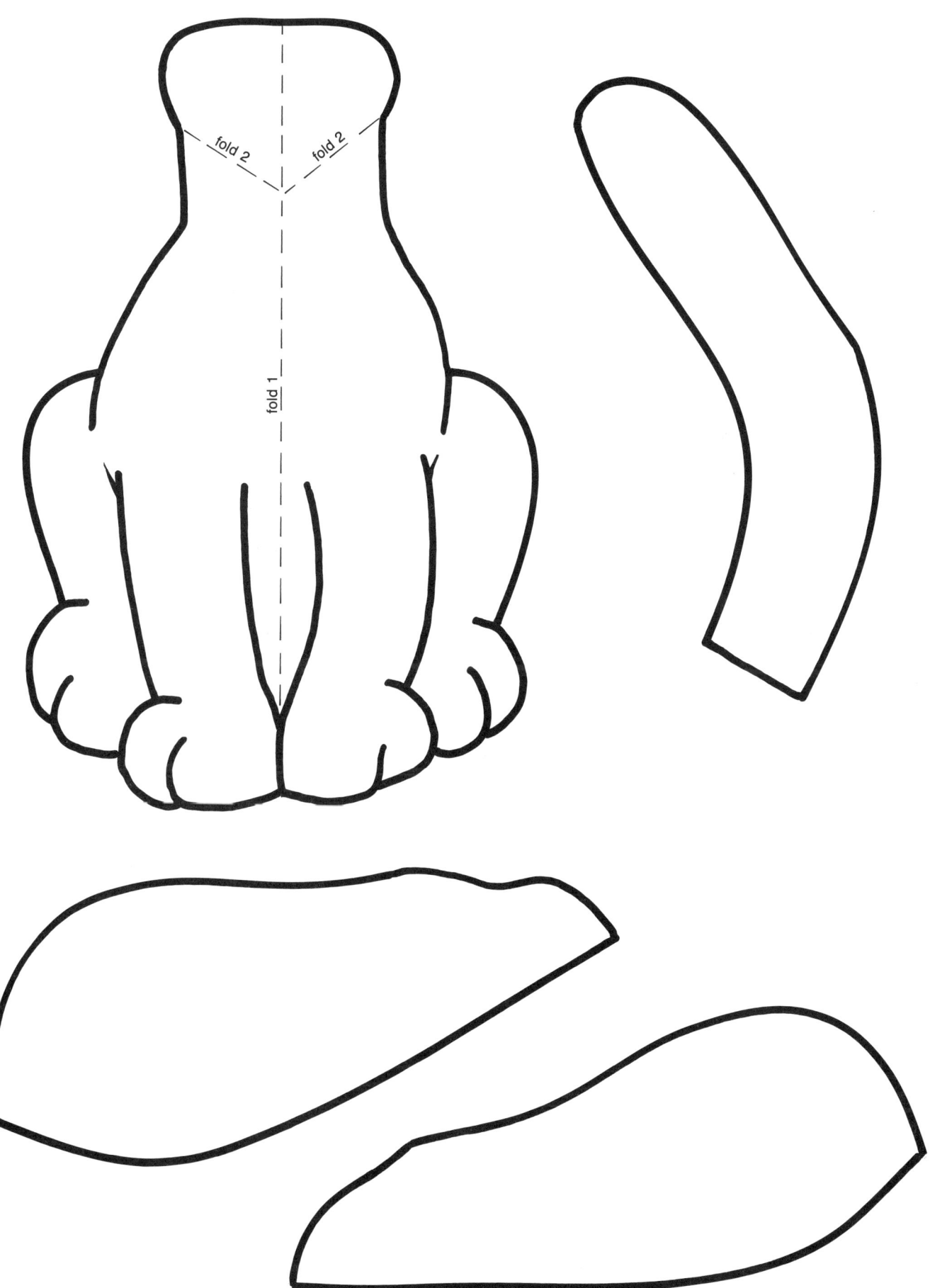

Mutt

1. Color the body parts.
2. Cut on the outside lines.
3. Head:
    a. Fold the head in half on fold 1. The colored side should be on the outside.
    b. Cut the nose and the ear lines while folded in half.
    c. Fold lines 2 and 3 while folded in half. Fold each line away from you and then again towards you.
    d. Unfold the head. Push the nose up between the ears until the heads folds flat.

push up

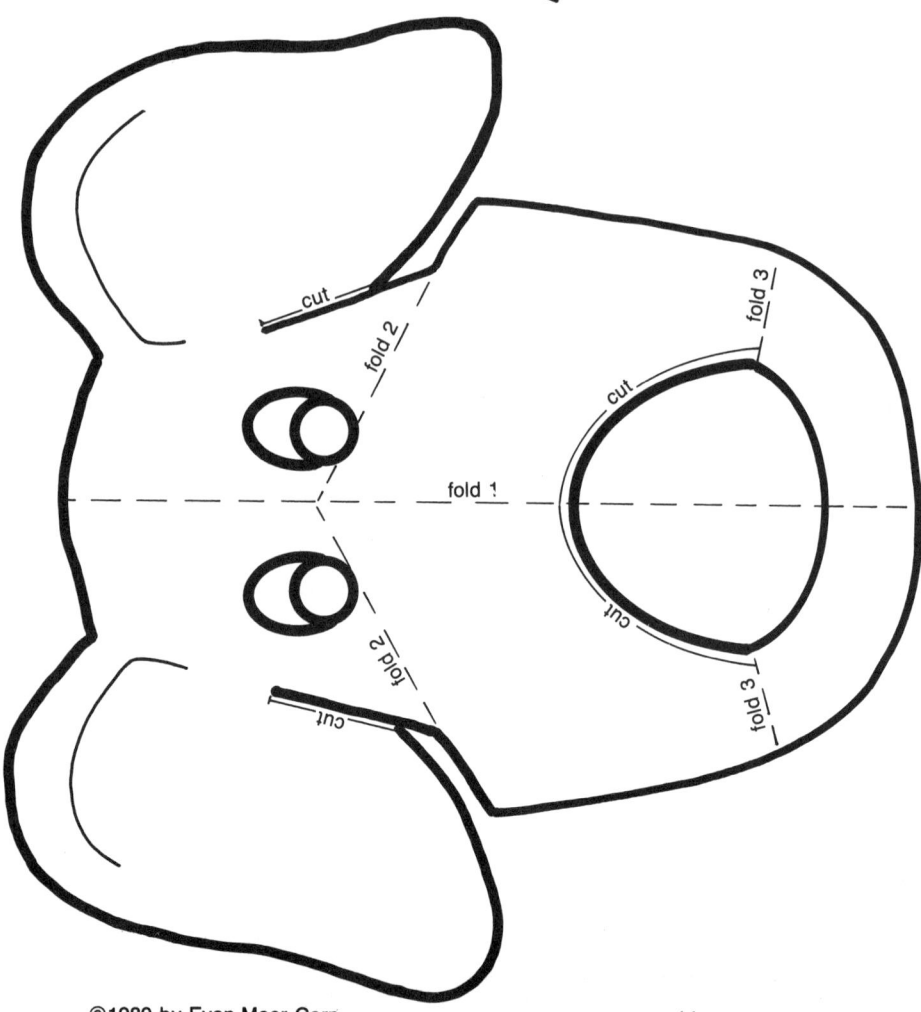

©1989 by Evan-Moor Corp.   Pop-Up Animals

4. Body:

   a. Fold the body in half on fold 1. The colored side should be on the outside.

   b. Make fold 2 while folded in half.

   c. Unfold the body. Reverse the folds and refold to the center. See picture.

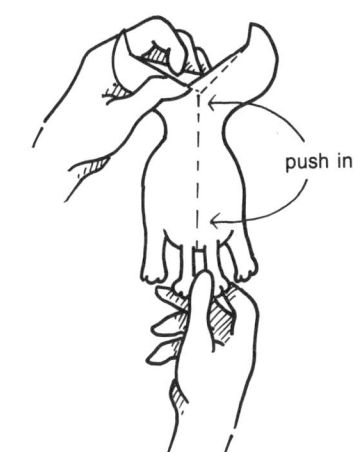

5. Glue the head and body to the background paper.

   Head: Apply glue only above fold 2.

   Body: Apply glue only below fold 2.

   Glue the tail in place.

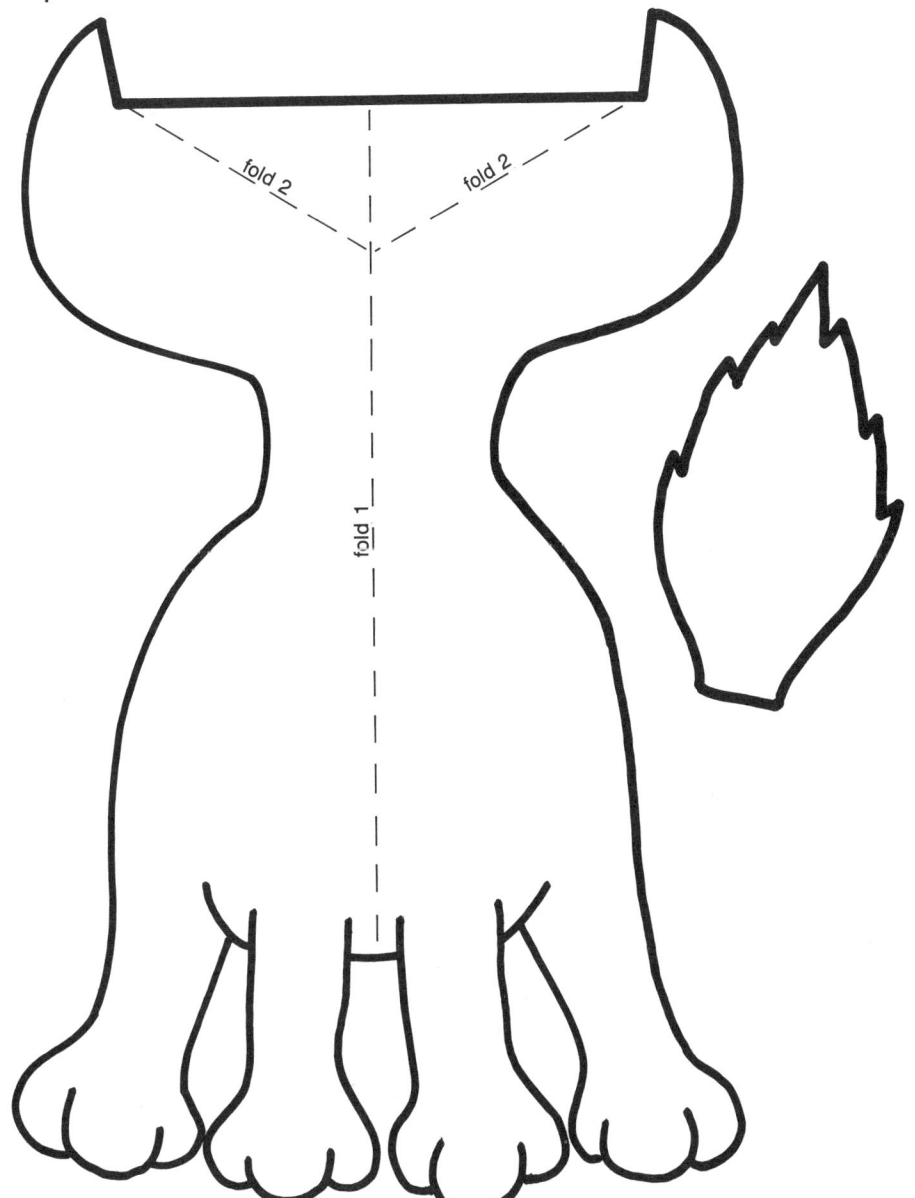

©1989 by Evan-Moor Corp.

Cat

1. Color the body parts.
2. Cut on the outside lines.
3. Head:
   a. Fold the head in half on fold 1. The colored side should be on the outside.
   b. Cut the nose line while folded in half.
      Cut the mouth lines while opened flat.
   c. Fold line 2 while folded in half. Fold each line away from you and then again towards you.

4. Body:
   a. Fold the body in half on fold 1. The colored side should be on the outside.
   b. Make fold 2 while folded in half.

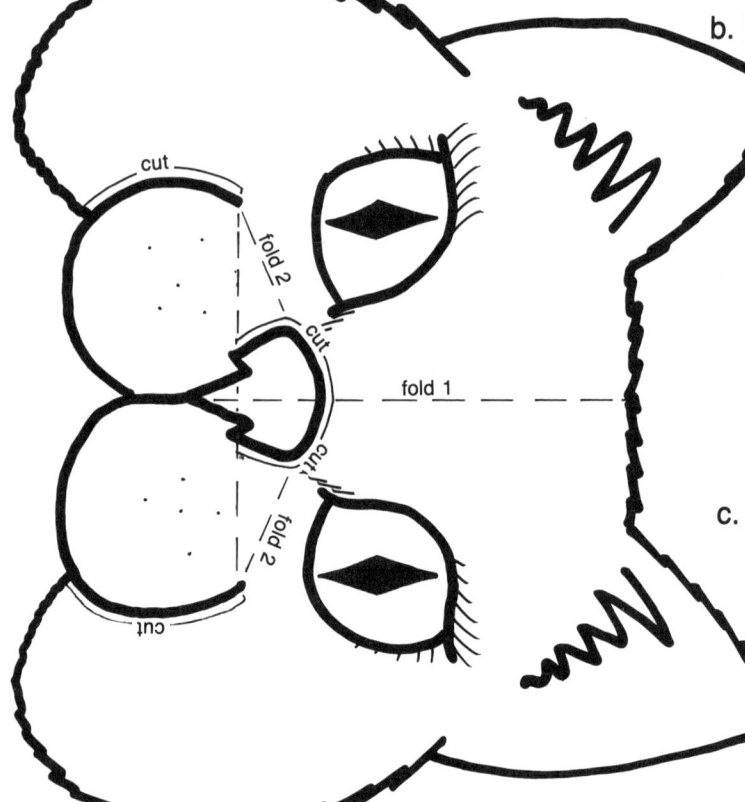

   c. Unfold the body. Reverse the folds and refold to the center. See picture.

©1989 by Evan-Moor Corp.   Pop-Up Animals

5. Glue the head and body to the background paper.

   Head: Apply glue only above fold 2.

   Body: Apply glue only below fold 2.

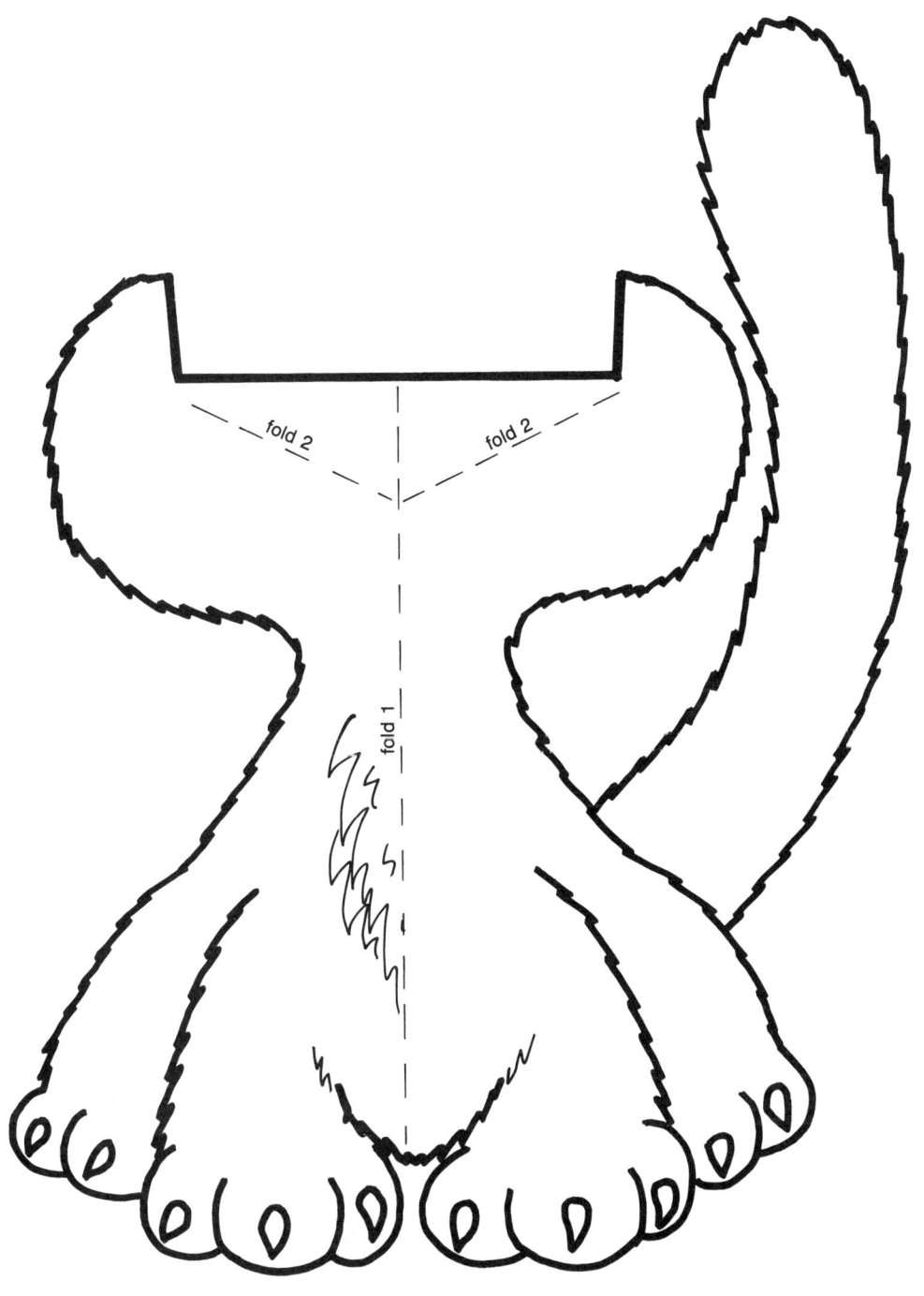

Bunny

1. Color the body parts.
2. Cut on the outside lines.
3. Head:
   a. Fold the head in half on fold 1. The colored side should be on the outside.
   b. Cut the nose line while folded in half.
   c. Fold lines 2 and 3 while folded in half. Fold each line away from you and then again towards you.
   d. Unfold the head. Push the nose up between the ears until the head folds flat.

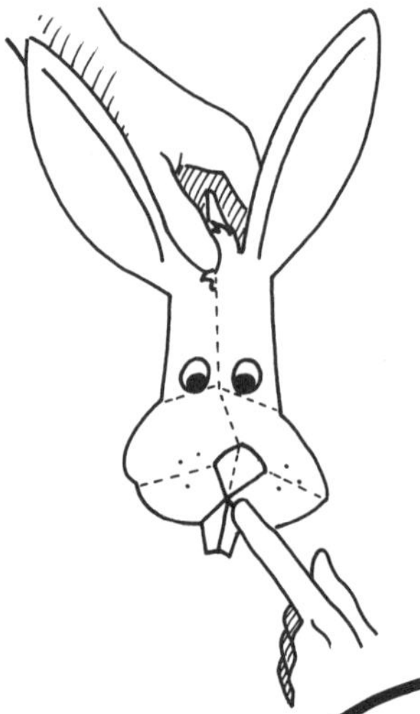

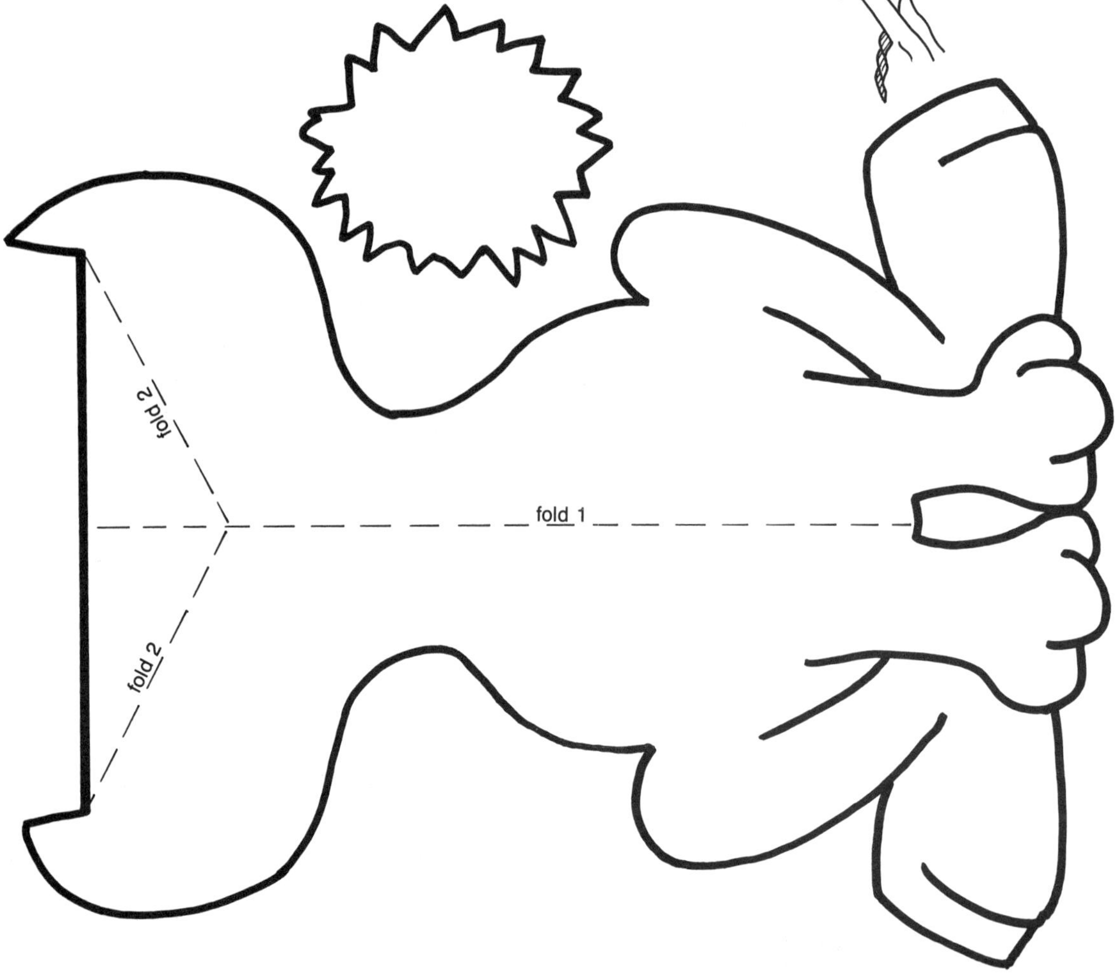

fold 2

fold 1

fold 2

©1989 by Evan-Moor Corp.   Pop-Up Animals

4. Body

   a. Fold the body in half on fold 1. The colored side should be on the outside.

   b. Make fold 2 while folded in half.

   c. Unfold the body. Reverse the folds and refold to the center. See picture.

5. Glue the head and body to the background paper.

   Head: Apply glue only above fold 2.

   Body: Apply glue only below fold 2.

   Glue the tail in place.

©1989 by Evan-Moor Corp.

Pop-Up Animals

Donkey

1. Color the body parts.
2. Cut on the outside lines.
3. Head:
   a. Fold the head in half on fold 1. The colored side should be on the outside.
   b. Fold lines 2 and 3 while folded in half. Fold each line away from you and then again towards you.
   c. Unfold the head. Push the nose up between the ears until the head folds flat.

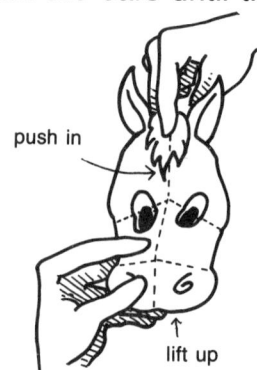

4. Body:
   a. Fold the body in half on fold 1. The colored side should be on the outside.
   b. Make fold 2 while folded in half.
   c. Unfold the body. Reverse the folds and refold to the center. See picture.

©1989 by Evan-Moor Corp.

5. Glue the head and body to the background paper.

   Head: Apply glue only above fold 2.

   Body: Apply glue only below fold 2.

   Glue tail in place.

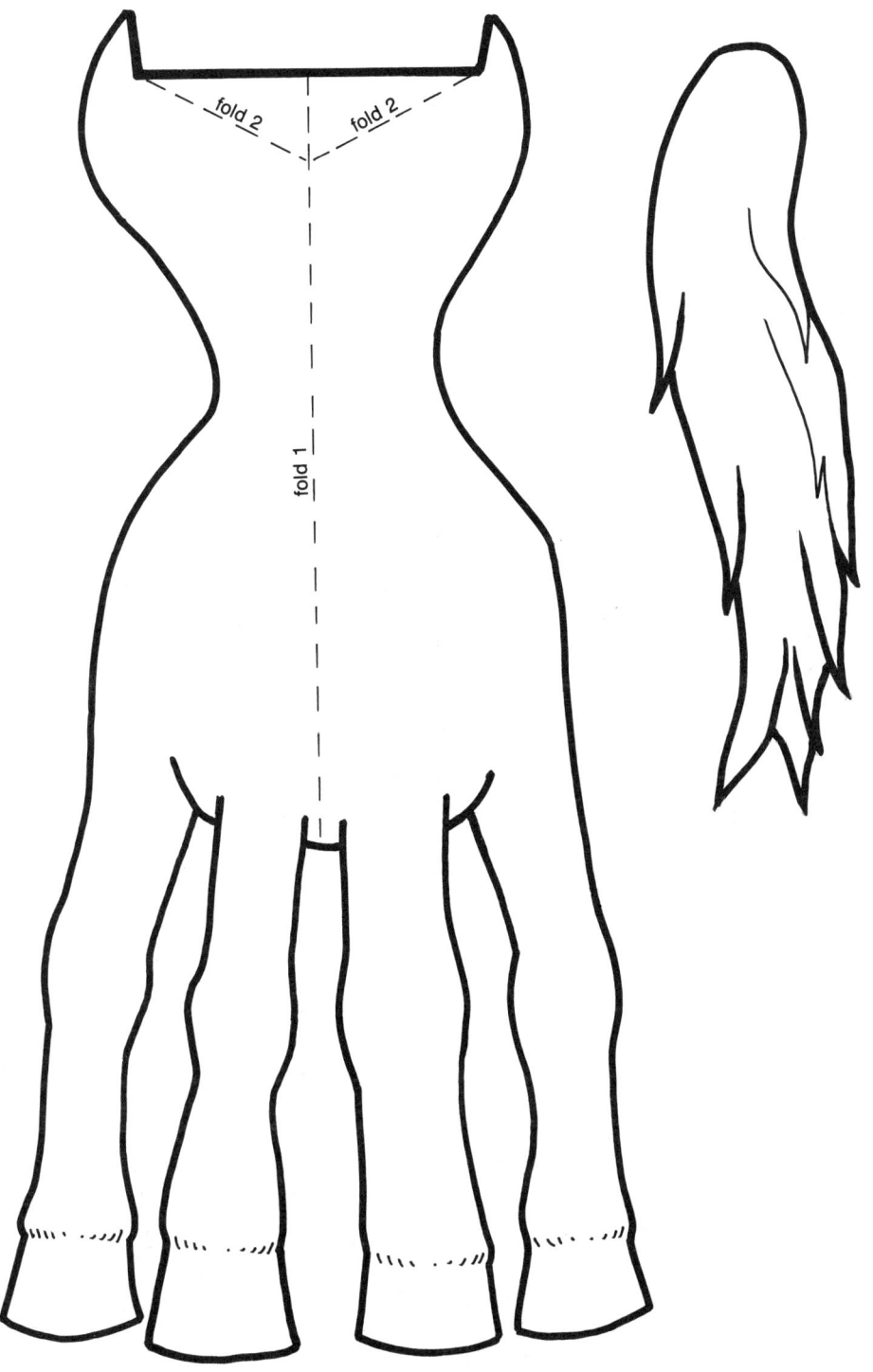

Cow

1. Color the body parts.
2. Cut on the outside lines.
3. Head:
   a. Fold the head in half on fold 1. The colored side should be on the outside.
   b. Fold lines 2 and 3 while folded in half. Fold each line away from you and then again towards you.
   c. Unfold the head. Push the nose up between the ears until the head folds flat.

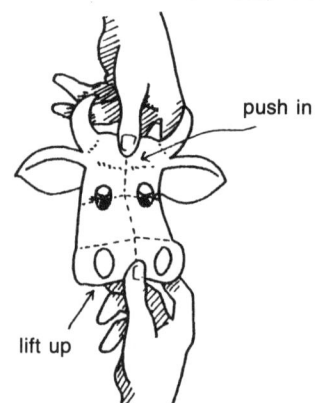

4. Body:
   a. Fold the body in half on fold 1. The colored side should be on the outside.
   b. Make fold 2 while folded in half.
   c. Unfold the body. Reverse the folds and refold to the center. See picture.

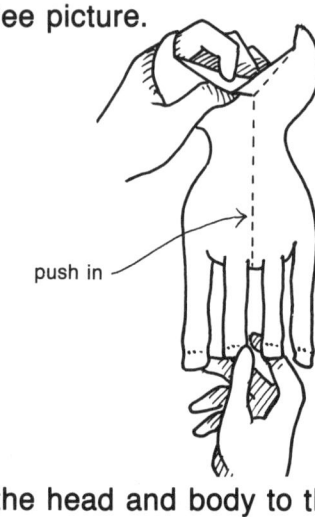

5. Glue the head and body to the background paper.

   Head: Apply glue only above fold 2.

   Body: Apply glue only below fold 2.

   Glue tail in place.

©1989 by Evan-Moor Corp.   Pop-Up Animals

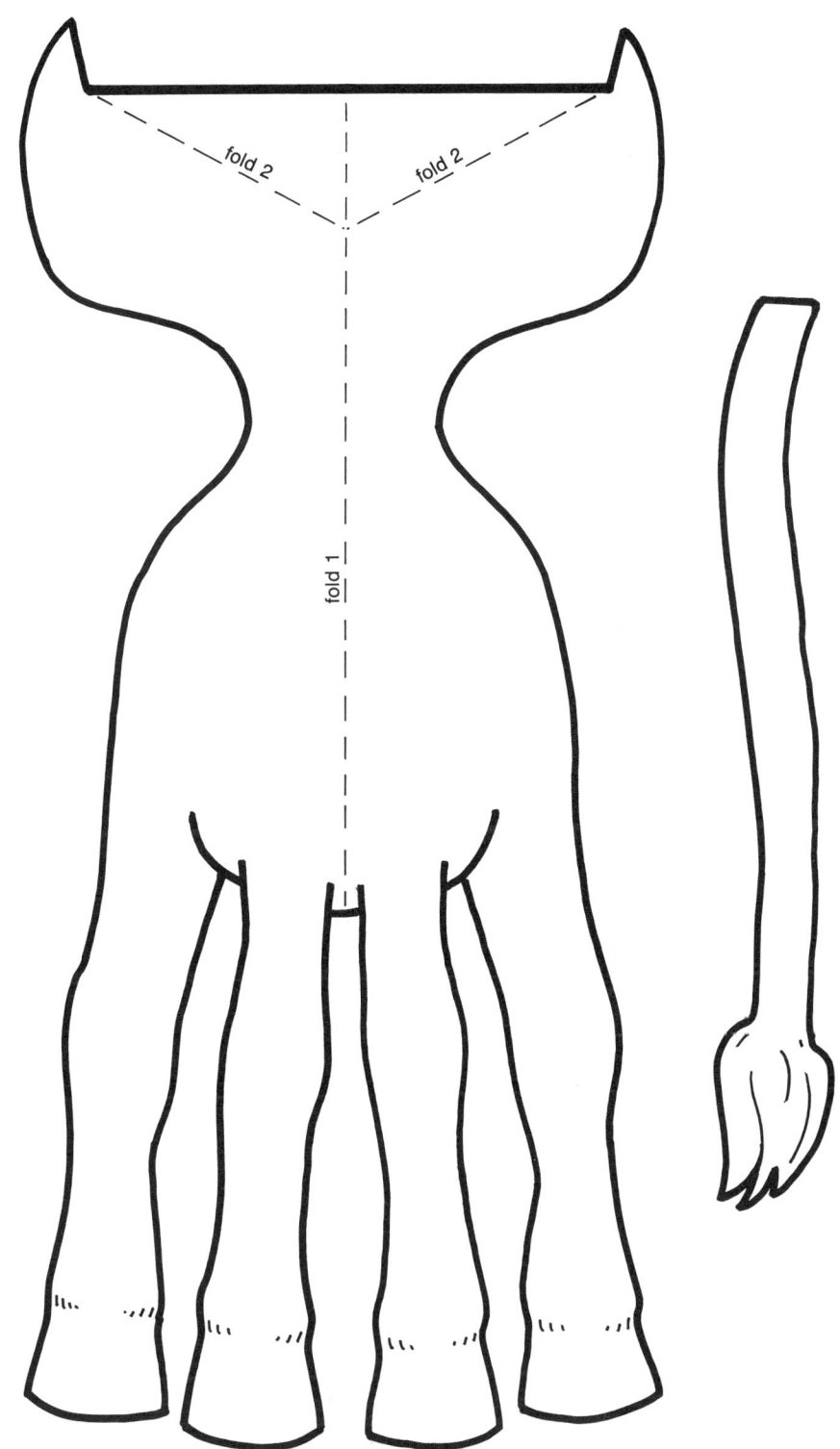

Frog

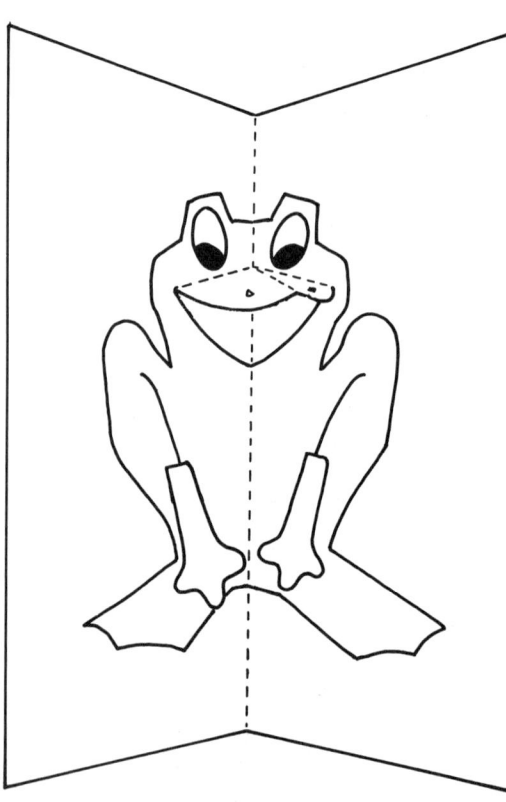

1. Color the body parts.
2. Cut on the outside lines.
3. Body:
    a. Fold the body in half on fold 1. The colored side should be on the outside.
    b. Cut the mouth line while folded in half.
    c. Fold line 2 while folded in half. Fold each line away from you and then again towards you.
    d. Unfold the body. Push the mouth up between the eyes until the frog folds flat.

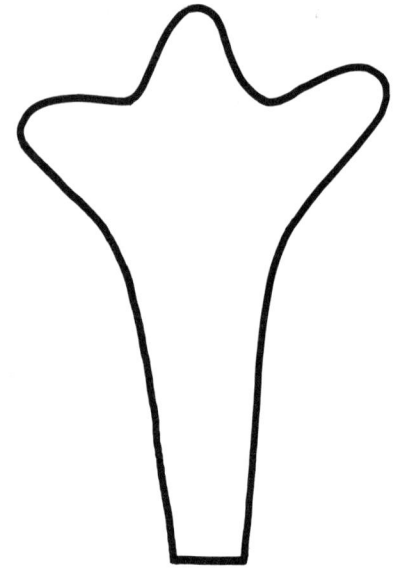

4. Glue the frog to the background paper. Apply glue only to the frog's body, not to his mouth. Glue the front feet in place.

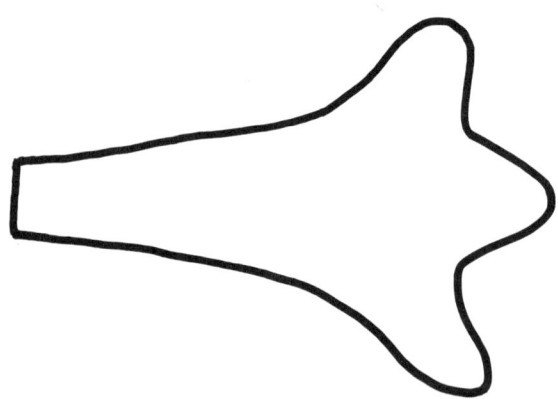

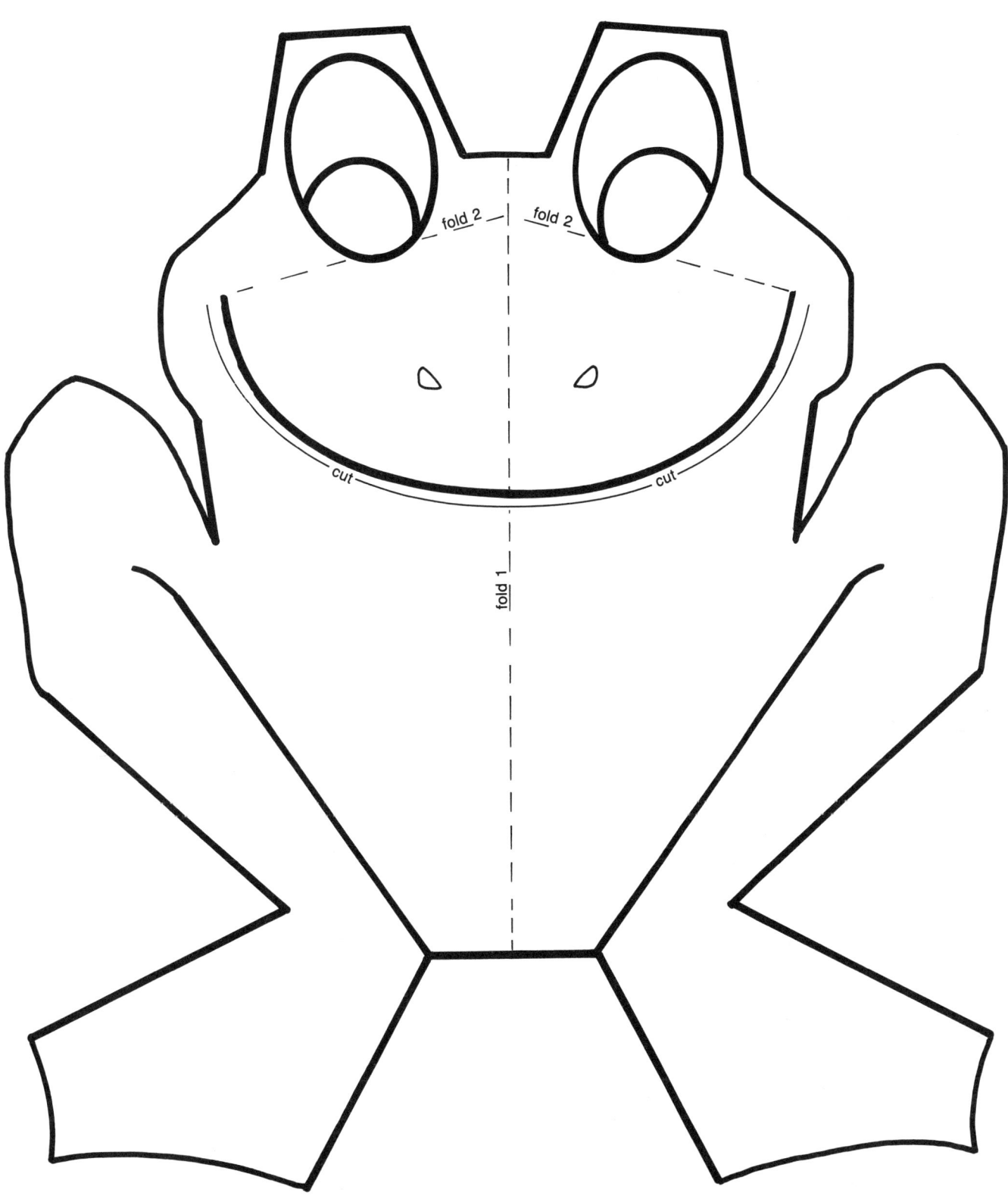

Sheep

1. Color the body parts.
2. Cut the outside lines.
3. Head:
   a. Fold the head in half on fold 1. The colored side should be on the outside.
   b. Fold lines 2 and 3 while folded in half. Fold each line away from you and then again towards you.
   c. Unfold the head. Push the nose up between the ears until the head folds flat.

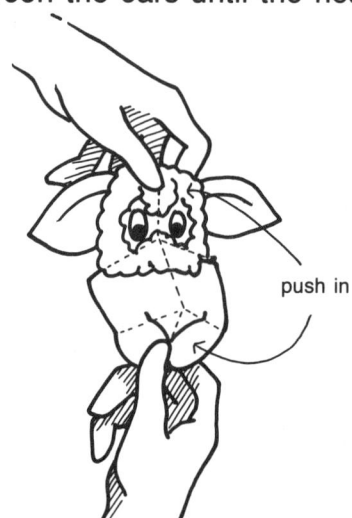
push in

4. Body:
   a. Fold the body in half on fold 1. The colored side should be on the outside.
   b. Make fold 2 while folded in half.
   c. Unfold the body. Reverse the folds and refold to the center. See picture.

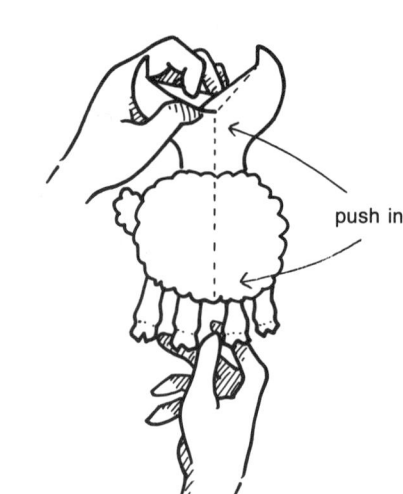
push in

©1989 by Evan-Moor Corp.

5. Glue the head and body to the background paper.

   Head: Apply glue only above fold 2.

   Body: Apply glue only below fold 2.

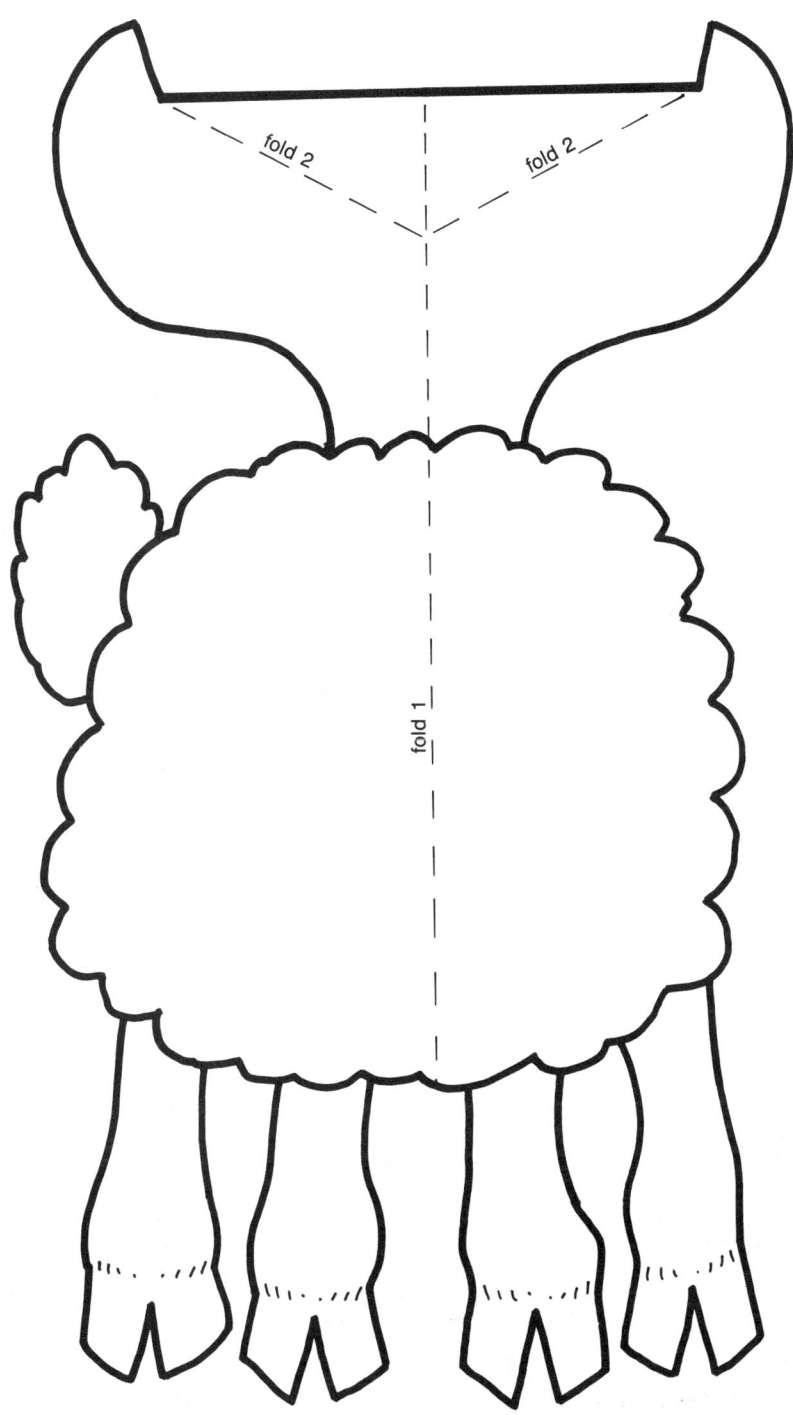

©1989 by Evan-Moor Corp. 27 Pop-Up Animals

Duck

1. Color the body parts. Color both sides (inside and outside) of the beak.
2. Cut on the outside lines.
3. Head:
   a. Fold the head in half on fold 1. The printed side should be on the outside.
   b. Cut the beak lines.
   c. Fold on line 2 while folded in half. Fold each line away from you and then again towards you.
   d. Unfold the head. Reverse the fold on the beak and push it up until it folds flat.

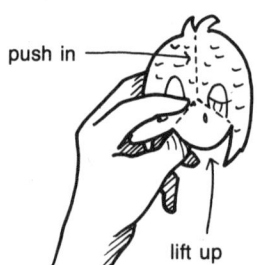

4. Body:
   a. Fold the body in half on fold 1. The printed side should be on the outside.
   b. Make fold 2 while folded in half.
   c. Unfold the body. Reverse folds and refold to the center. See picture.

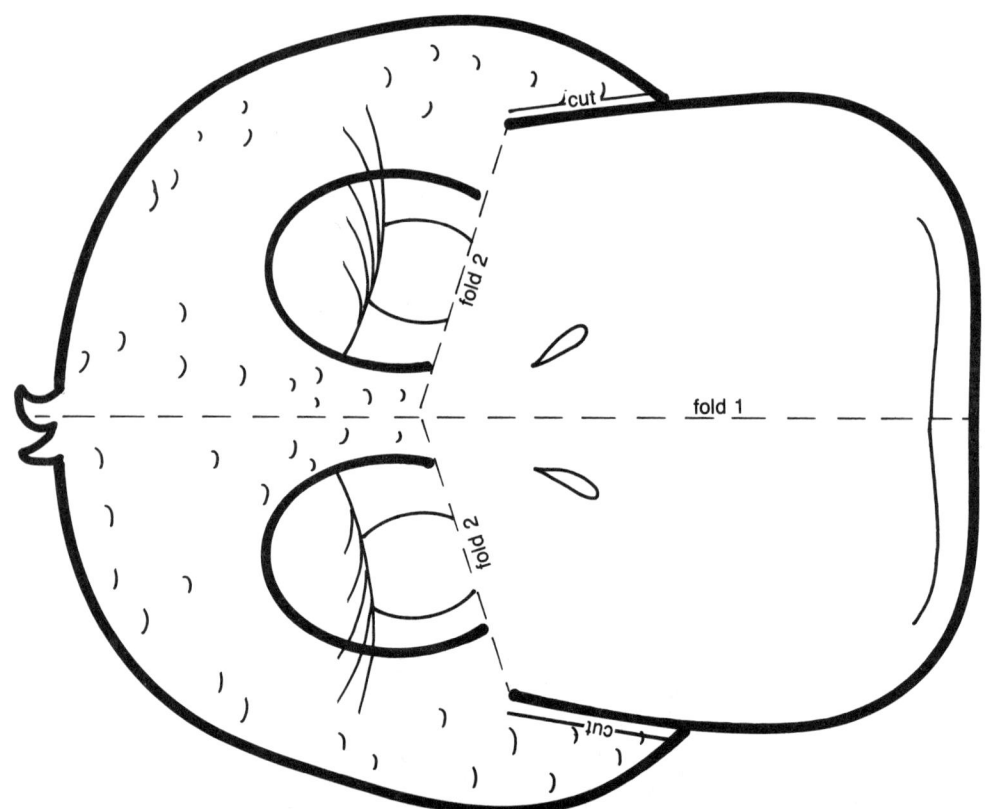

5. Glue the head and body to the background paper.
   Head: Apply glue only above fold 2.
   Body: Apply glue only below fold 2.

©1989 by Evan-Moor Corp. — Pop-Up Animals

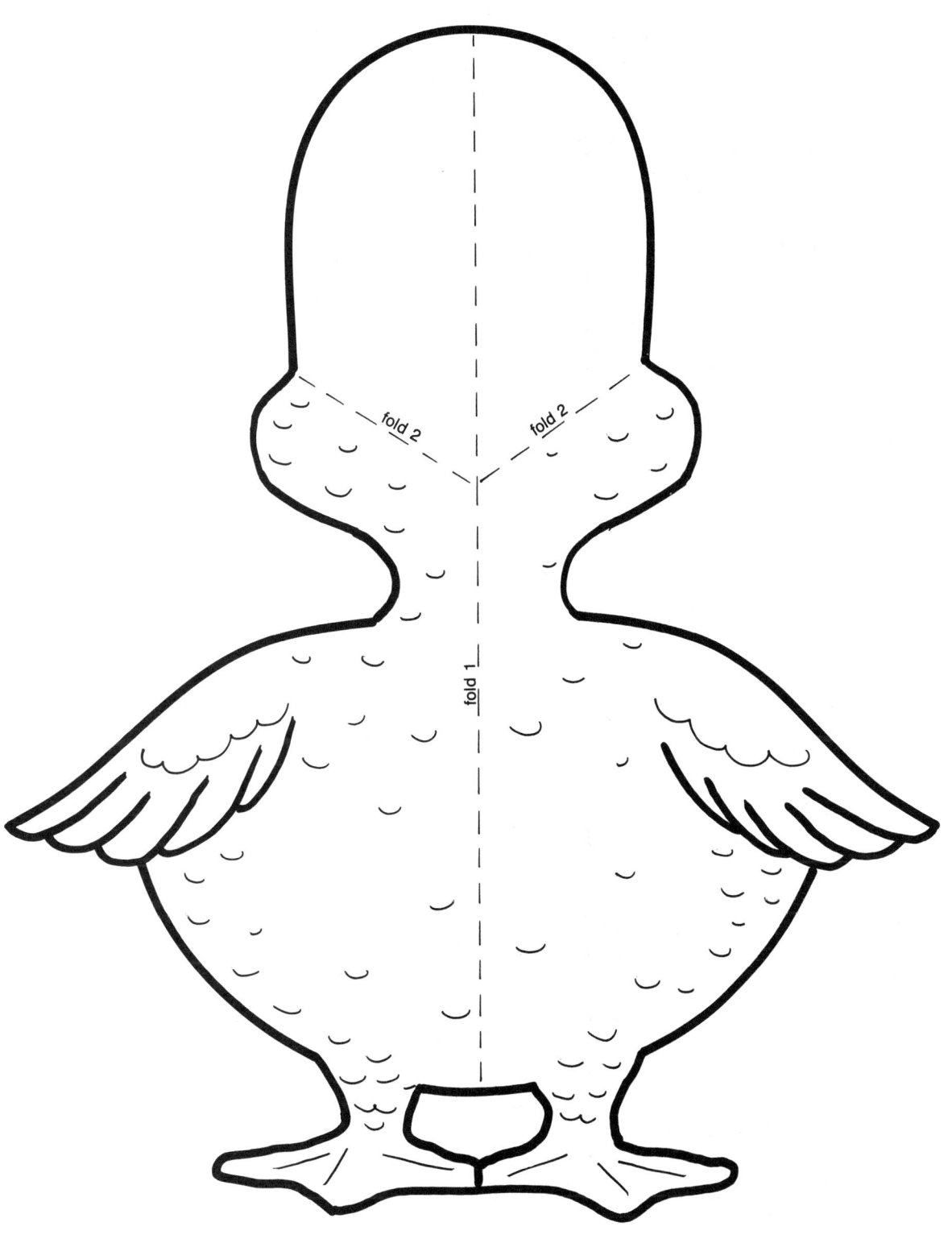

Optional: Color the inside of the duck's mouth red.

Owl

1. Color the body parts.
2. Cut the outside lines.
3. Head:
    a. Fold the head in half on fold 1. The colored side should be on the outside.
    b. Fold on line 2 while folded in half. Fold each line away from you and then again towards you.
    c. Unfold the head. Push the beak up until the head folds flat.

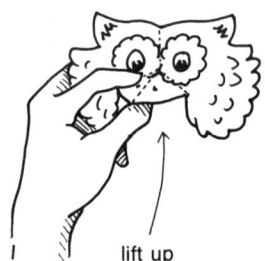
lift up

4. Body:
    a. Fold the body in half on fold 1. The colored side should be on the outside.
    b. Make fold 2 while folded in half.
    c. Unfold the body. Reverse the folds and refold to the center. See picture.

©1989 by Evan-Moor Corp.

5. Glue the head and body to the background paper.

   Head: Apply glue only above fold 2.

   Body: Apply glue only below fold 2.

Hen

1. Color the body parts.
2. Cut the outside lines.
3. Head:
   a. Fold the head in half on fold 1. The colored side should be on the outside.
   b. Fold on line 2 while folded in half. Fold each line away from you and then again towards you.
   c. Unfold the head. Push the beak up until the head folds flat.

lift up

4. Body:
   a. Fold the body in half on fold 1. The colored side should be on the outside.
   b. Make fold 2 while folded in half.
   c. Unfold the body. Reverse the folds and refold to the center. See picture.

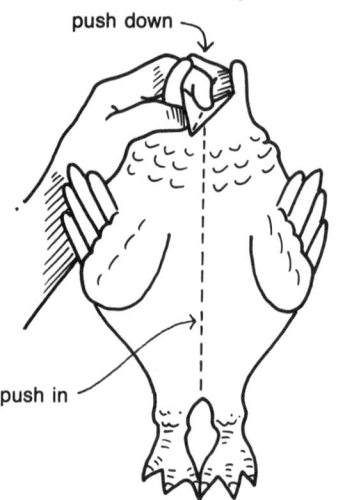
push down
push in

5. Glue the head and body to the background paper.

   Head: Apply glue only above fold 2.

   Body: Apply glue only below fold 2.

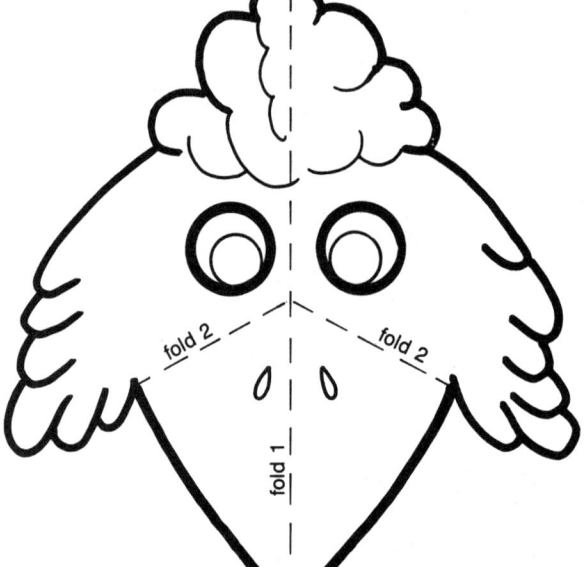

©1989 by Evan-Moor Corp. Pop-Up Animals

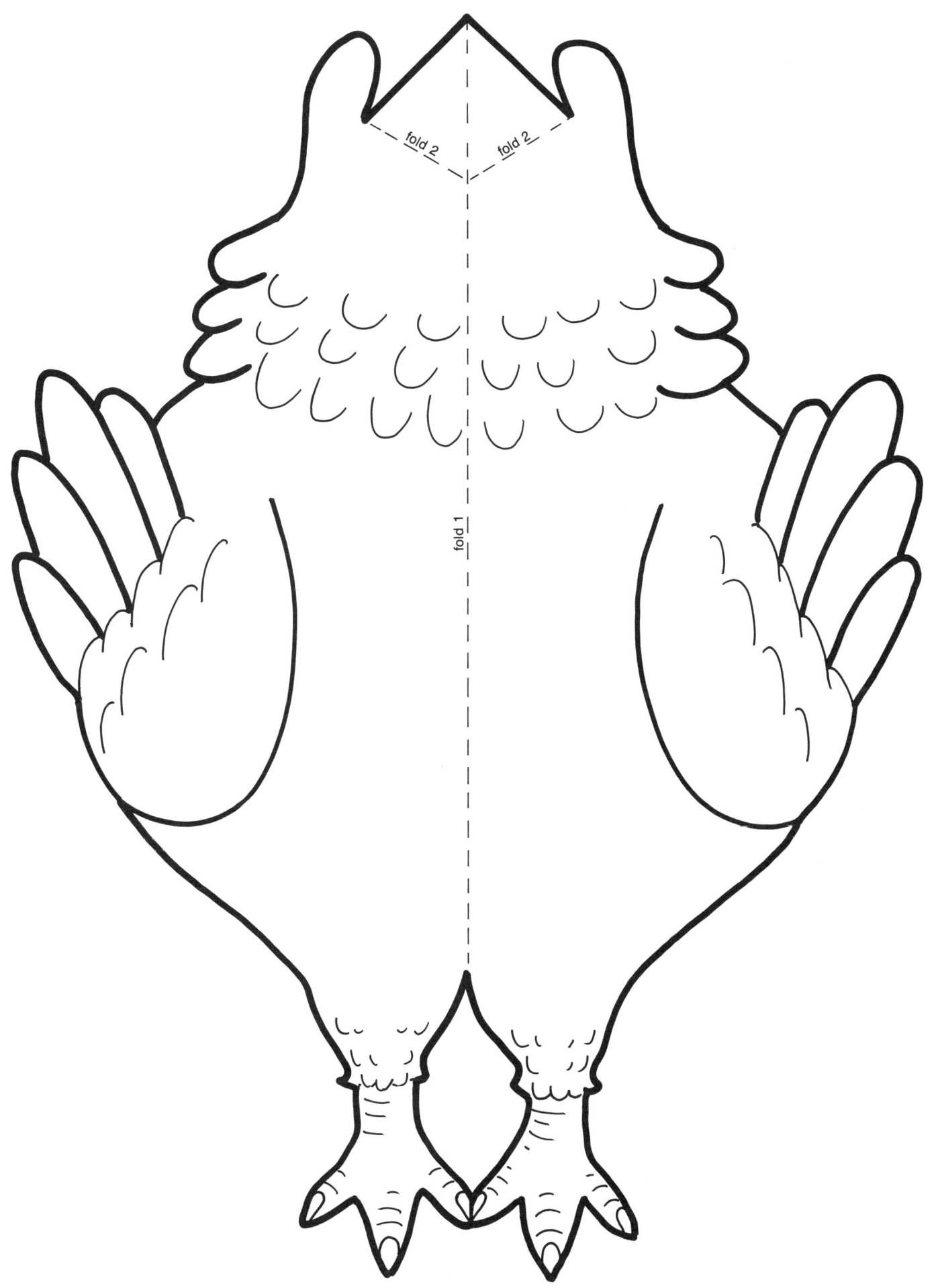

Penguin

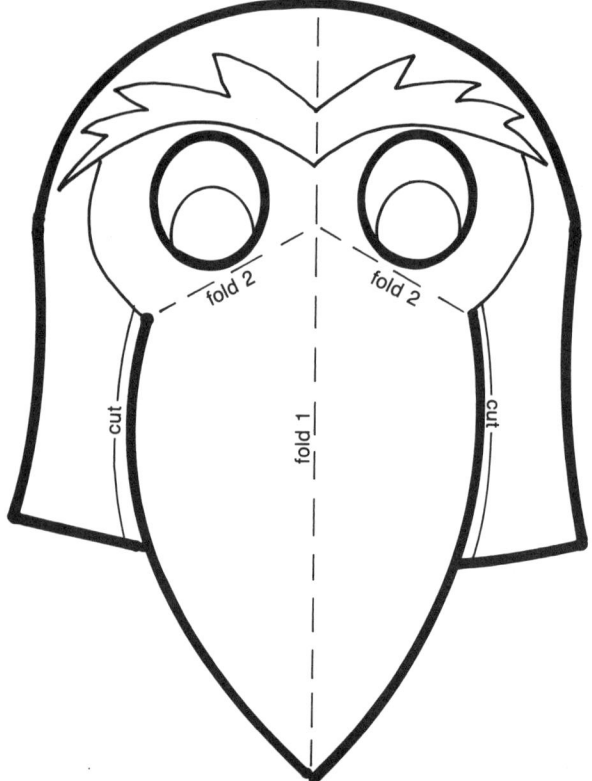

1. Color the body parts. Color both sides (inside and outside) of the beak.
2. Cut on the outside lines.
3. Head:
    a. Fold the head in half on fold 1. The printed side should be on the outside.
    b. Cut the beak lines.
    c. Fold on line 2 while folded in half. Fold each line away from you and then again towards you.
    d. Unfold the head. Reverse the fold on the beak and push it up until it folds flat.

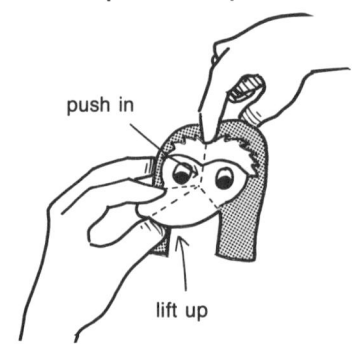

4. Body:
    a. Fold the body in half on fold 1. The printed side should be on the outside.
    b. Cut along the beak lines.
    c. Make fold 2 while folded in half.
    d. Unfold the body. Reverse the folds and refold to the center. See picture.

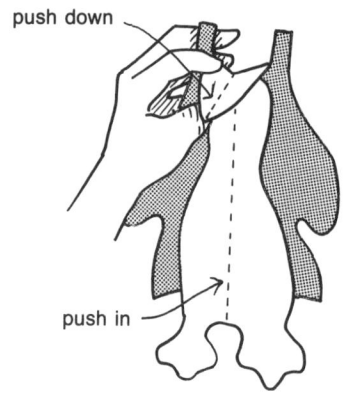

5. Glue the head and body to the background paper.

    Head: Apply glue only above fold 2.

    Body: Apply glue only below fold 2.

    Optional: Color the inside of the penguin's mouth red.

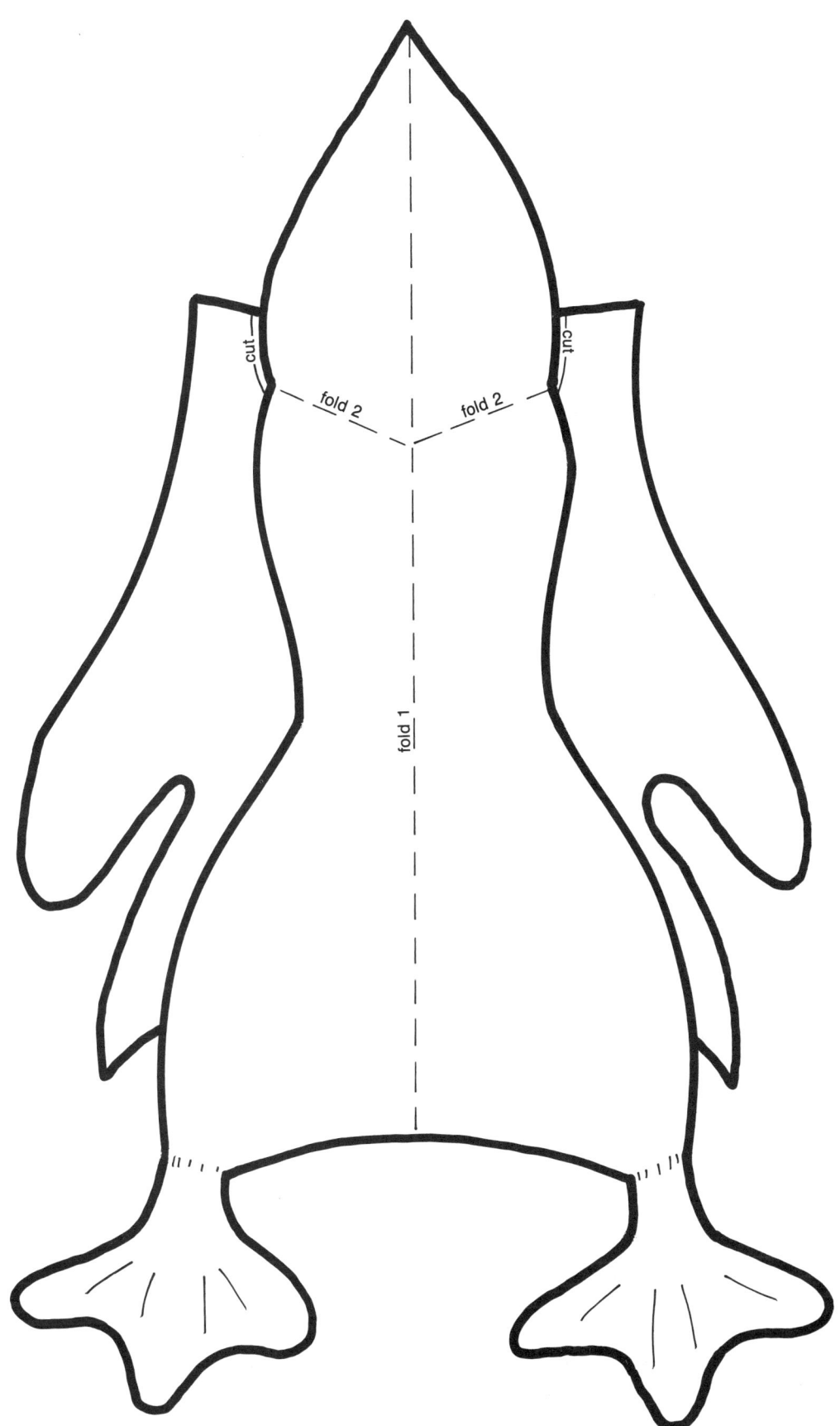

Bear

1. Color the body parts.
2. Cut on the outside lines.
3. Head:

   a. Fold the head in half on fold 1. The colored side should be on the outside.

   b. Cut the nose and mouth lines while folded in half.

   c. Fold lines 2 and 3 while folded in half. Fold each line away from you and then again towards you.

   d. Unfold the head. Push the nose up until the head folds flat.

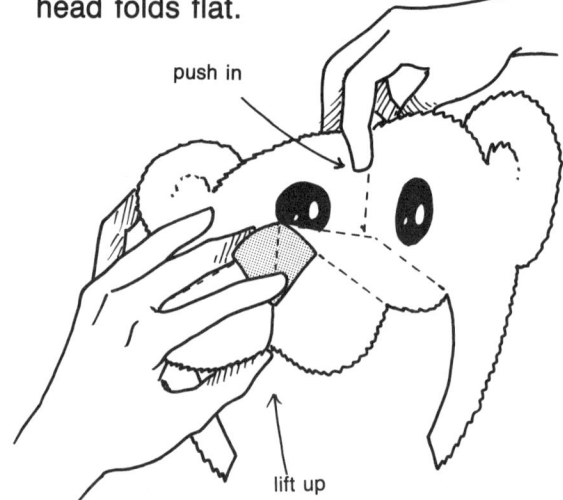

push in

lift up

4. Jaw:

   a. Fold the jaw in half on fold 1. The colored side should be on the outside.

   b. Cut the jaw lines.

   c. Make folds 2 and 3 while folded in half.

   d. Unfold the jaw. Reverse folds and refold to the center. See picture.

5. Glue the head and jaw to the background paper.

Head: Apply glue only above fold 2.

Jaw: Apply glue only below fold 2.

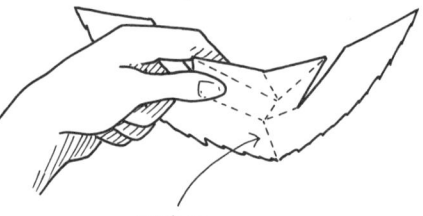

push in

©1989 by Evan-Moor Corp.

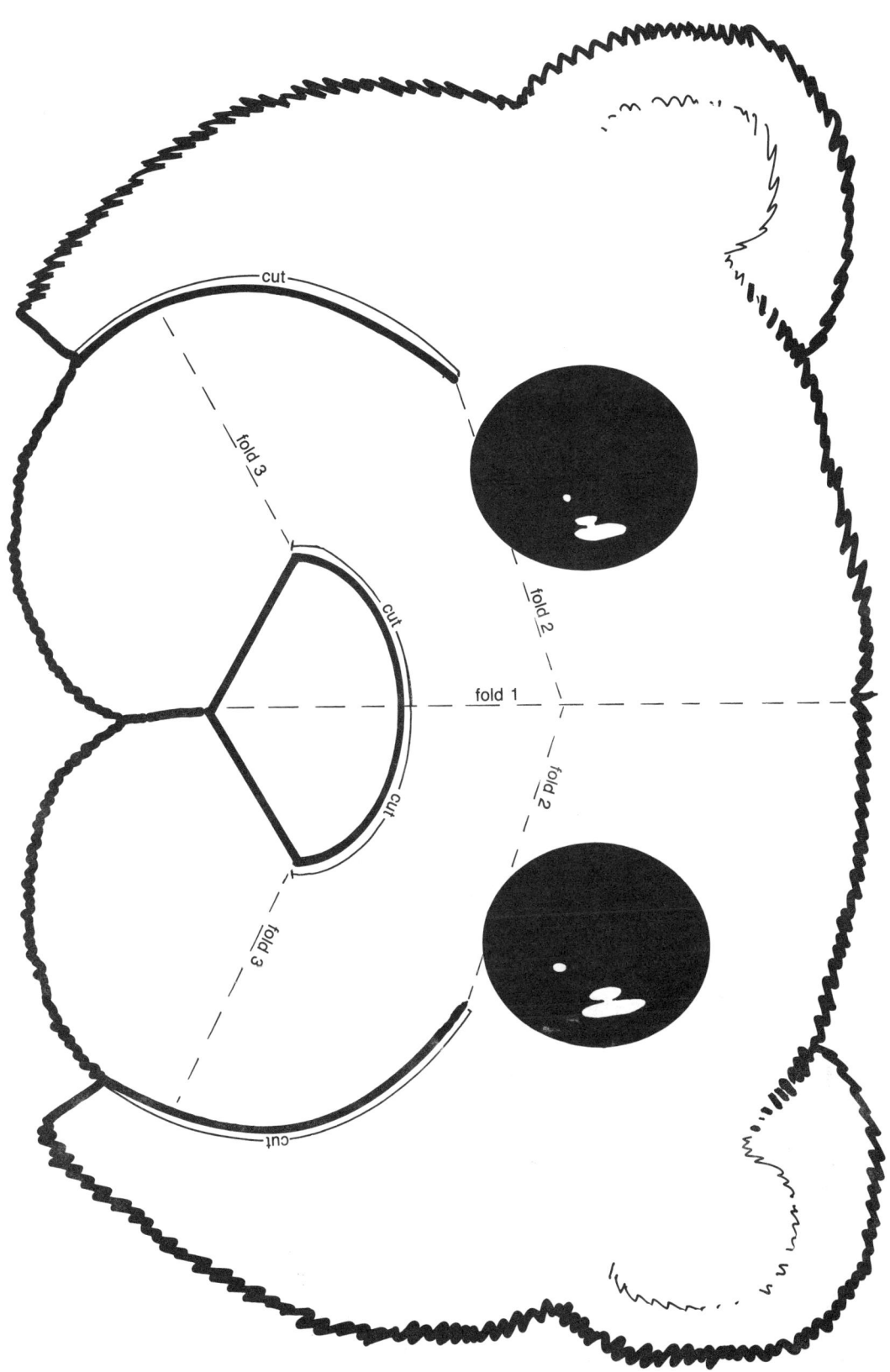

Reindeer

1. Color the body parts.
2. Cut on the outside lines.
3. Head:
   a. Fold the head in half on fold 1. The colored side should be on the outside.
   b. Cut the nose line while folded in half.
   c. Fold lines 2 and 3 while folded in half. Fold each line away from you and then again towards you.
   d. Unfold the head. Push the nose up between the ears until the head folds flat.

4. Body:
   a. Fold the body in half on fold 1. The colored side should be on the outside.
   b. Make fold 2 while folded in half.
   c. Unfold the body. Reverse the folds and refold to the center. See picture.

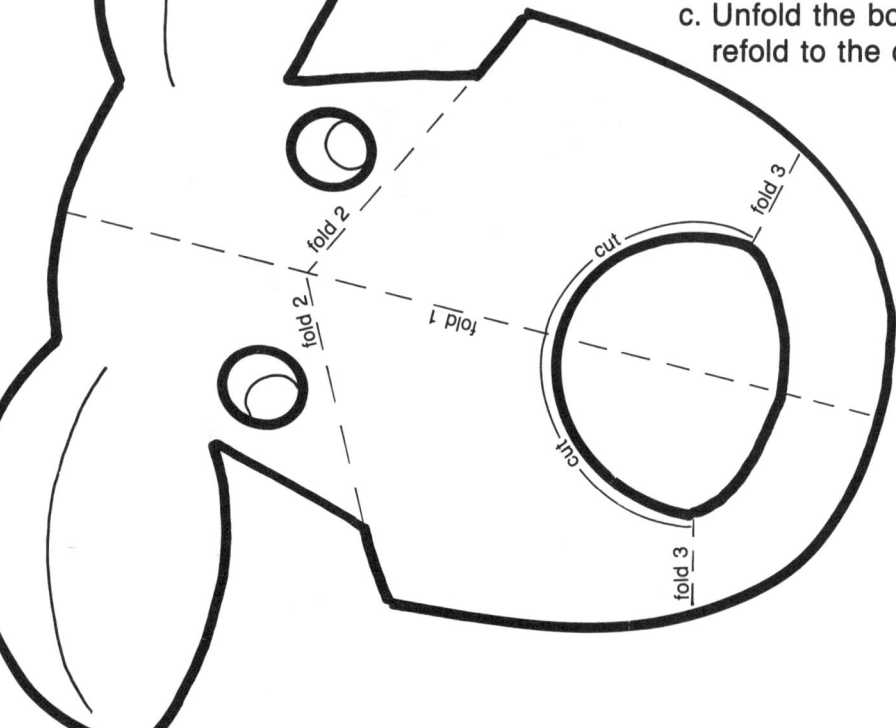

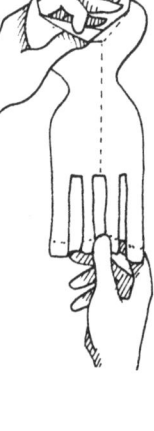

©1989 by Evan-Moor Corp.

5. Glue the head and body to the background paper.

   Head: Apply glue only above fold 2.

   Body: Apply glue only below fold 2.

   Glue the antlers and tail in place.

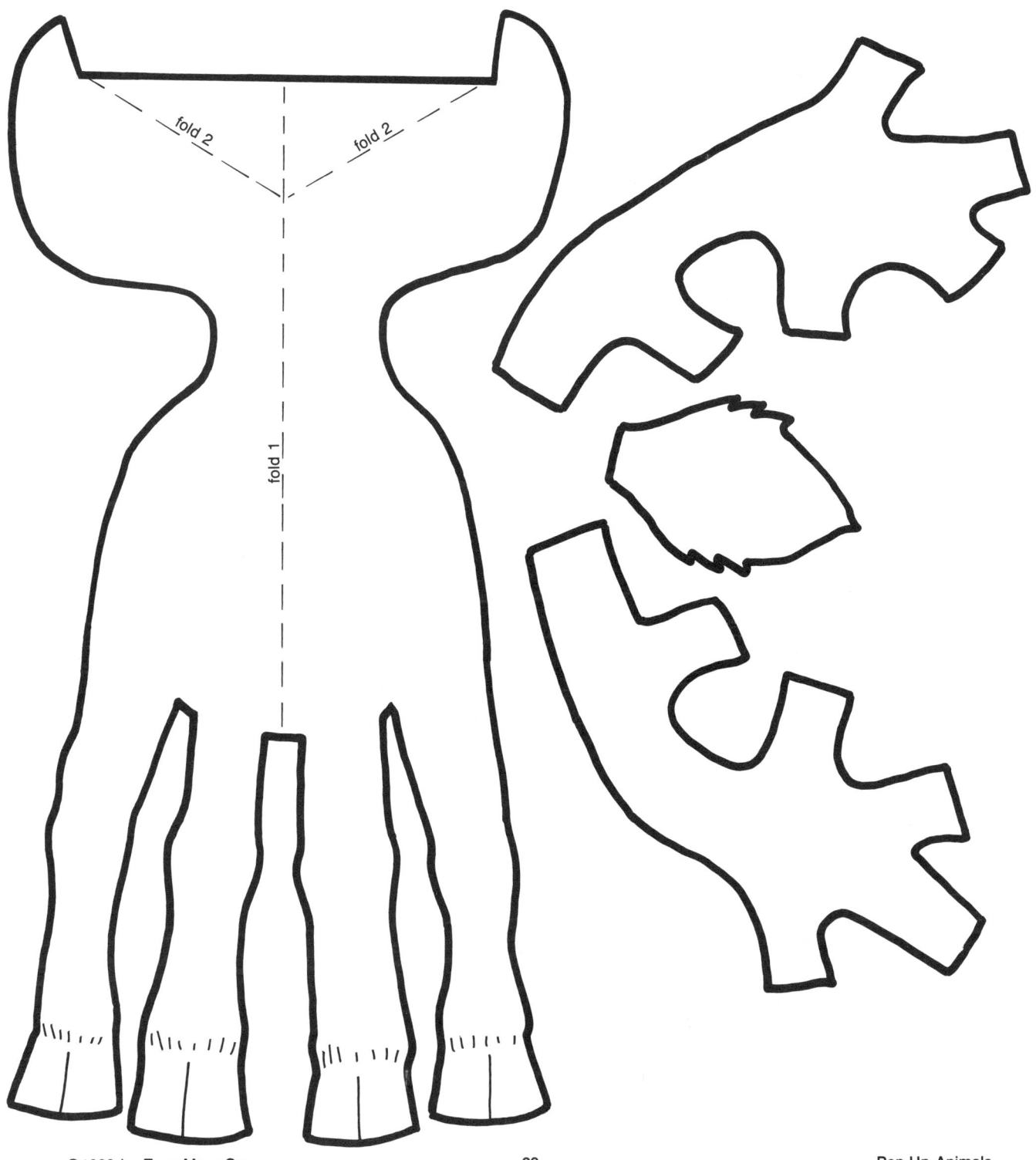

Kangaroo

1. Color the body parts.
2. Cut the outside lines.
3. Head:
   a. Fold the head in half on fold 1. The colored side should be on the outside.
   b. Cut the nose line while folded in half.
   c. Fold lines 2 and 3 while folded in half. Fold each line away from you and then again towards you.
   d. Unfold the head. Push the nose up until the head folds flat.

4. Upper Body and Lower Body
   a. Fold the body in half on fold 1. The colored side should be on the outside.
   b. Make fold 2 while folded in half.
   c. Unfold the body. Reverse the folds and refold to the center. See picture.

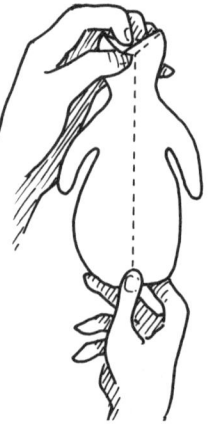

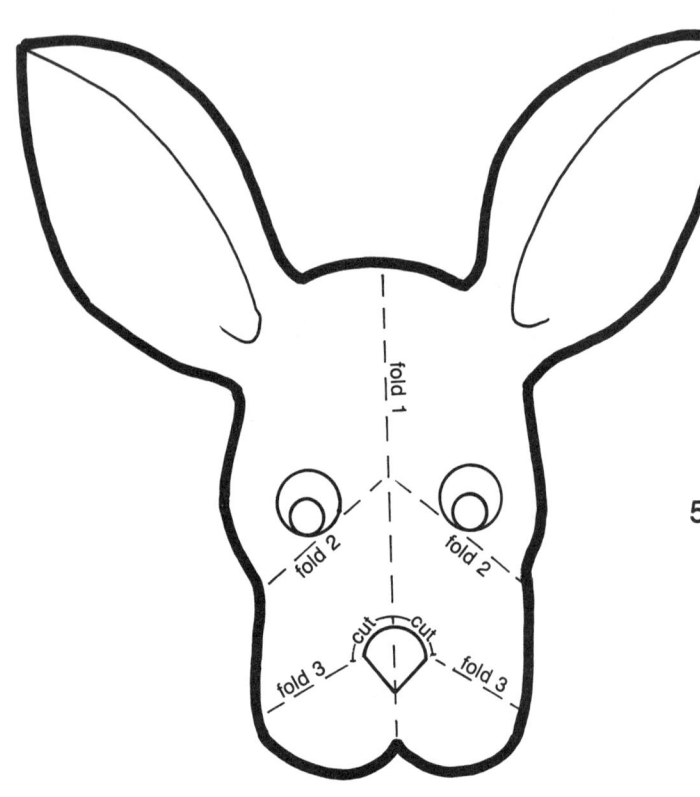

5. Glue the head, upper and lower body to the background paper.

   Head: Apply glue only above fold 2.

   Upper and Lower Body: Apply glue only below fold 2.

   Glue the tail in place.

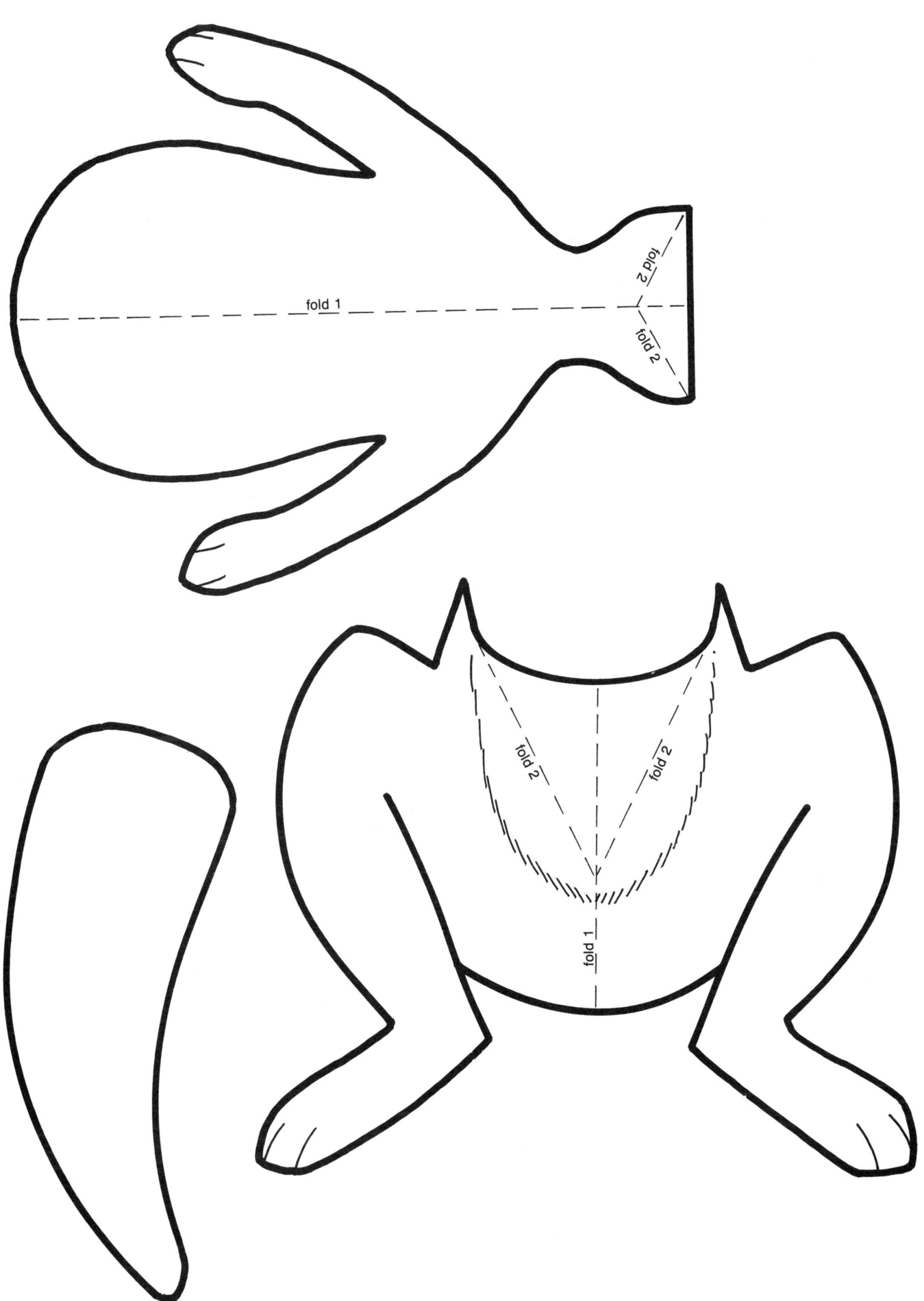

Pop-Up Animals

Lion

1. Color the body parts.
2. Cut on the outside lines.
3. Head:
   a. Fold the head in half on fold 1. The colored side should be on the outside.
   b. Cut the nose and mouth lines while folded in half.
   c. Fold lines 2 and 3 while folded in half. Fold each line away from you and then again towards you.

4. Body:
   a. Fold the body in half on fold 1. The colored side should be on the outside.
   b. Cut the mouth line.
   c. Make folds 2 and 3 while folded in half.
   d. Unfold the body. Reverse folds and refold to the center.

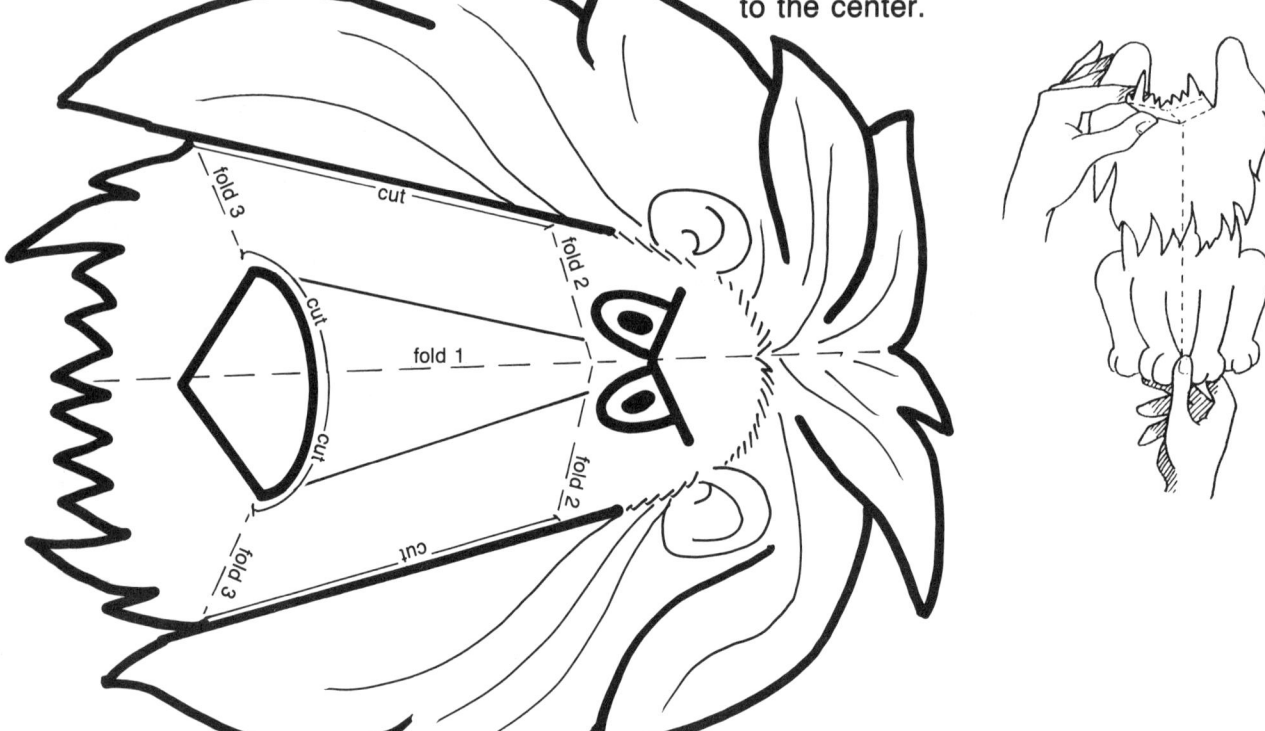

©1989 by Evan-Moor Corp. — Pop-Up Animals

5. Glue the head and body to the background paper.

   Head: Apply glue only above fold 2.

   Body: Apply glue only below fold 2.

   Optional: Color the inside of the lion's mouth red.

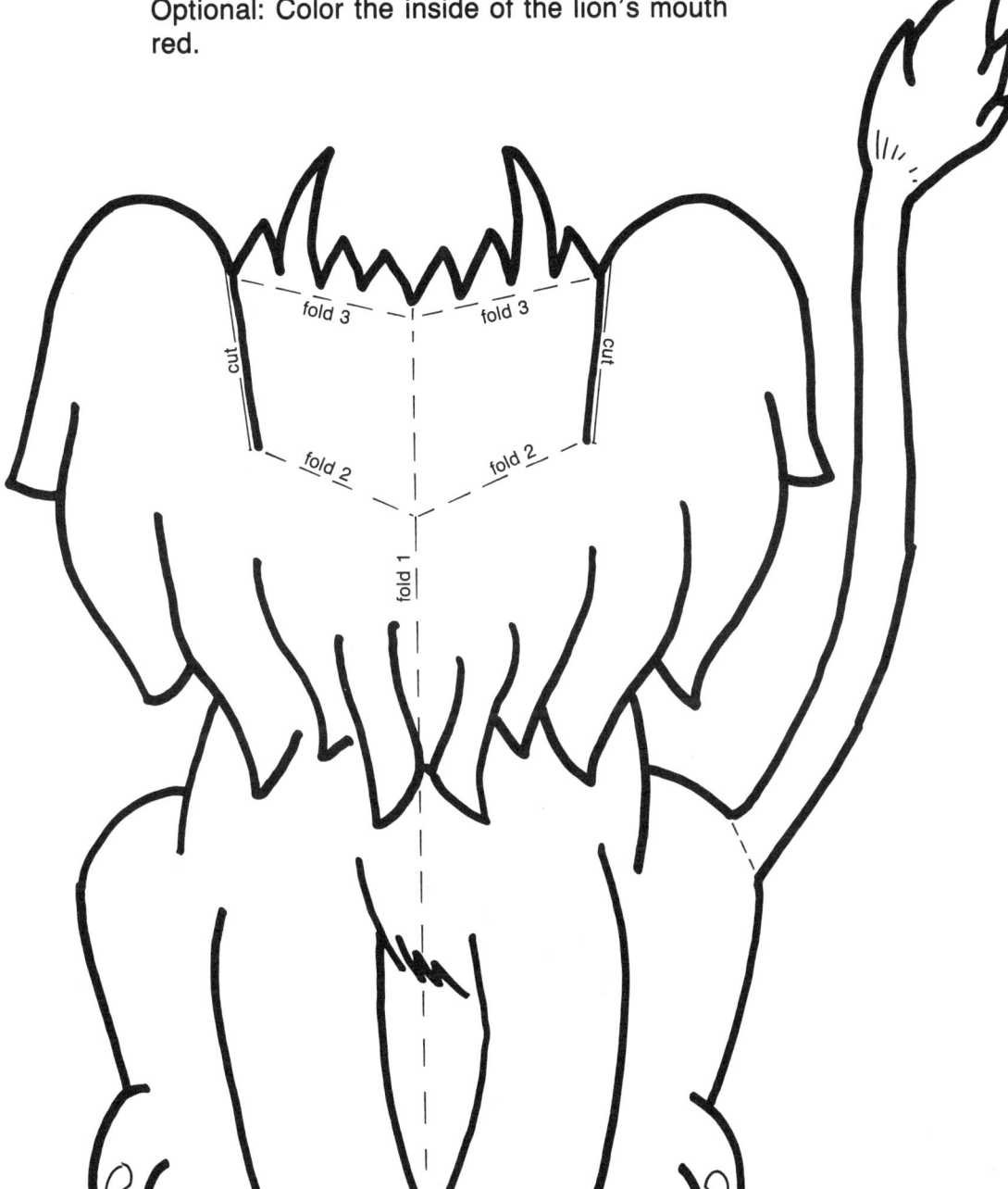

Dragon

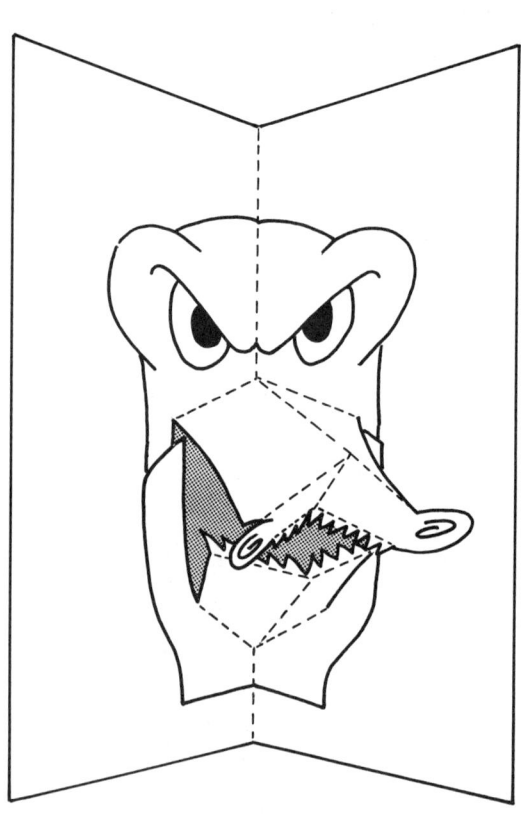

1. Color the body parts.
2. Cut on the outside lines.
3. Head:
   a. Fold the head in half on fold 1. The colored side should be on the outside.
   b. Cut the snout lines.
   c. Fold lines 2, 3 and 4 while folded in half. Fold each line away from you and then again towards you.
   d. Unfold the head. Push the nose up until the head folds flat.

4. Jaw:
   a. Fold the jaw in half on fold 1. The colored side should be on the outside.
   b. Cut the jaw lines.
   c. Make folds 2 and 3 while folded in half.
   d. Unfold the jaw. Reverse the folds and refold to the center. See picture.

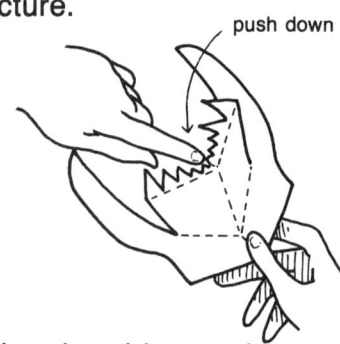

5. Glue the head and jaw to the background paper.

   Head: Apply glue only above fold 2.

   Jaw: Apply glue only below fold 2.

©1989 by Evan-Moor Corp.   Pop-Up Animals

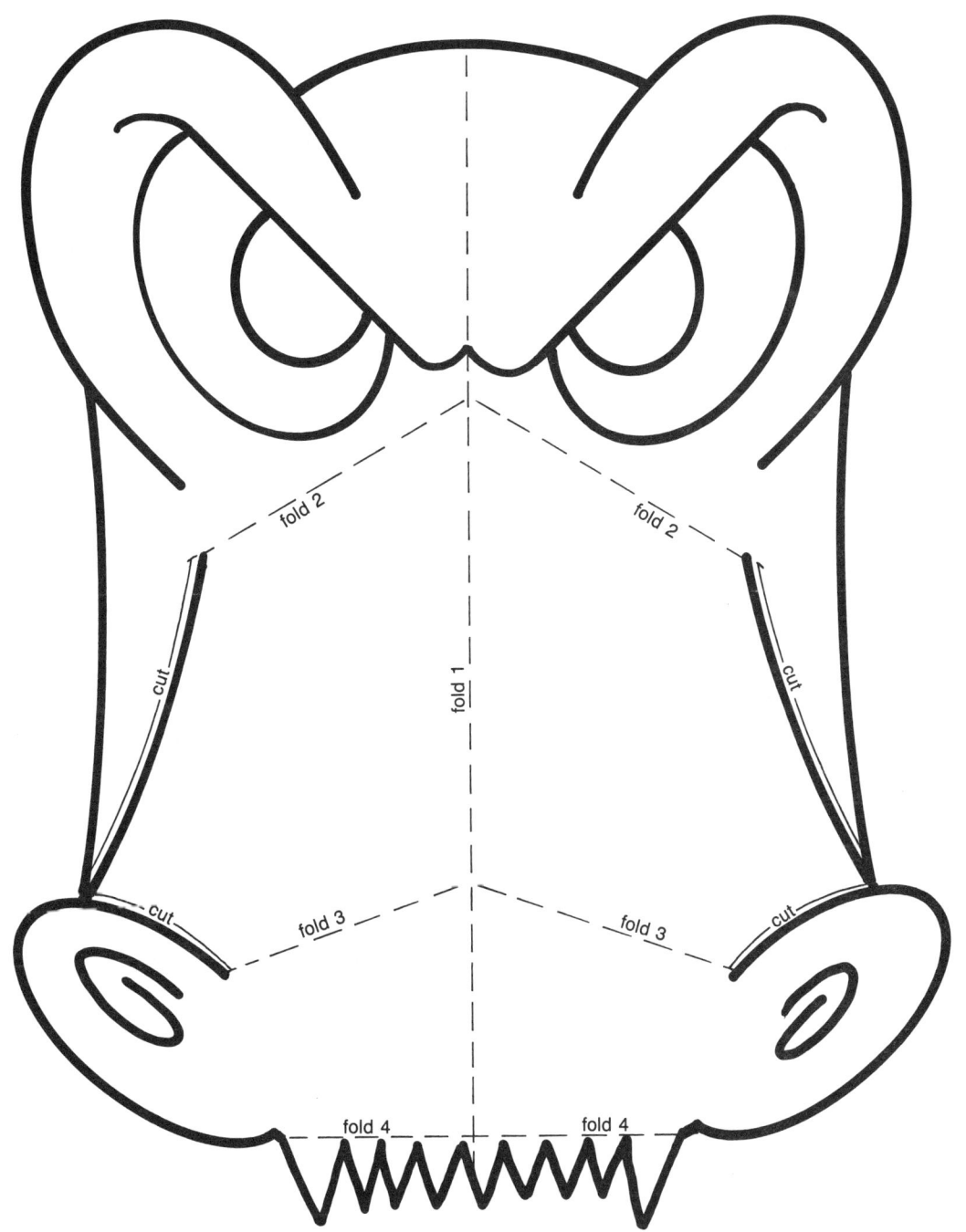

Rhinocerous

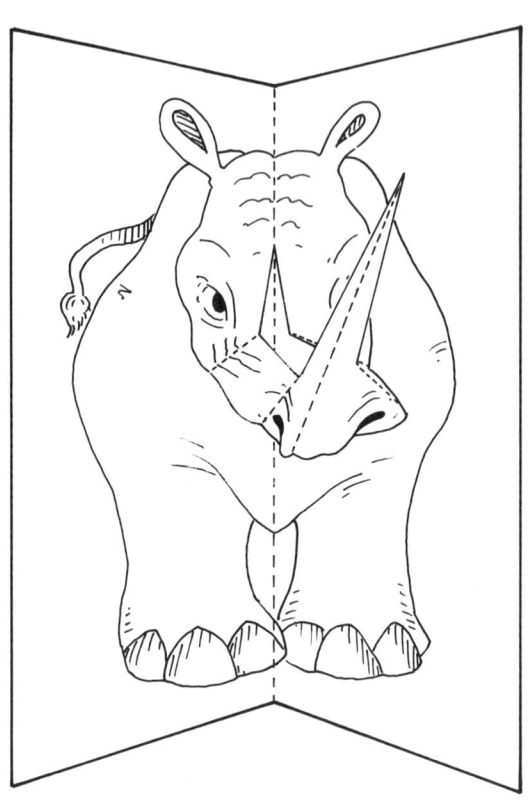

1. Color the body parts.

2. Cut on the outside lines.

3. Head:

    a. Fold the head in half on fold 1. The colored side should be on the outside.

    b. Cut the horn lines.

    c. Fold lines 2 and 3 while folded in half. Fold each line away from you and then again towards you.

    d. Unfold the head. Push the nose up until the head folds flat.

4. Fold the body in half on fold 1.

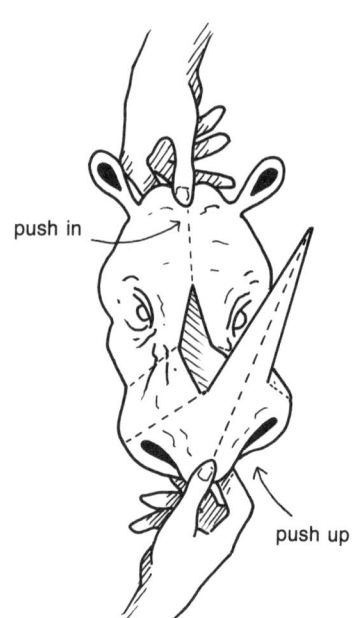

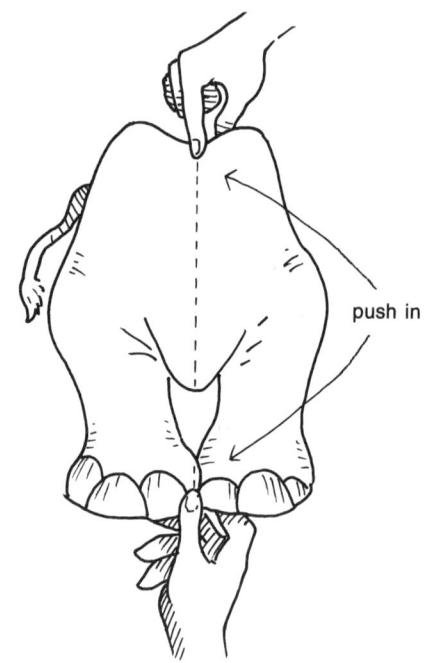

5. Glue the head and body to the background paper.

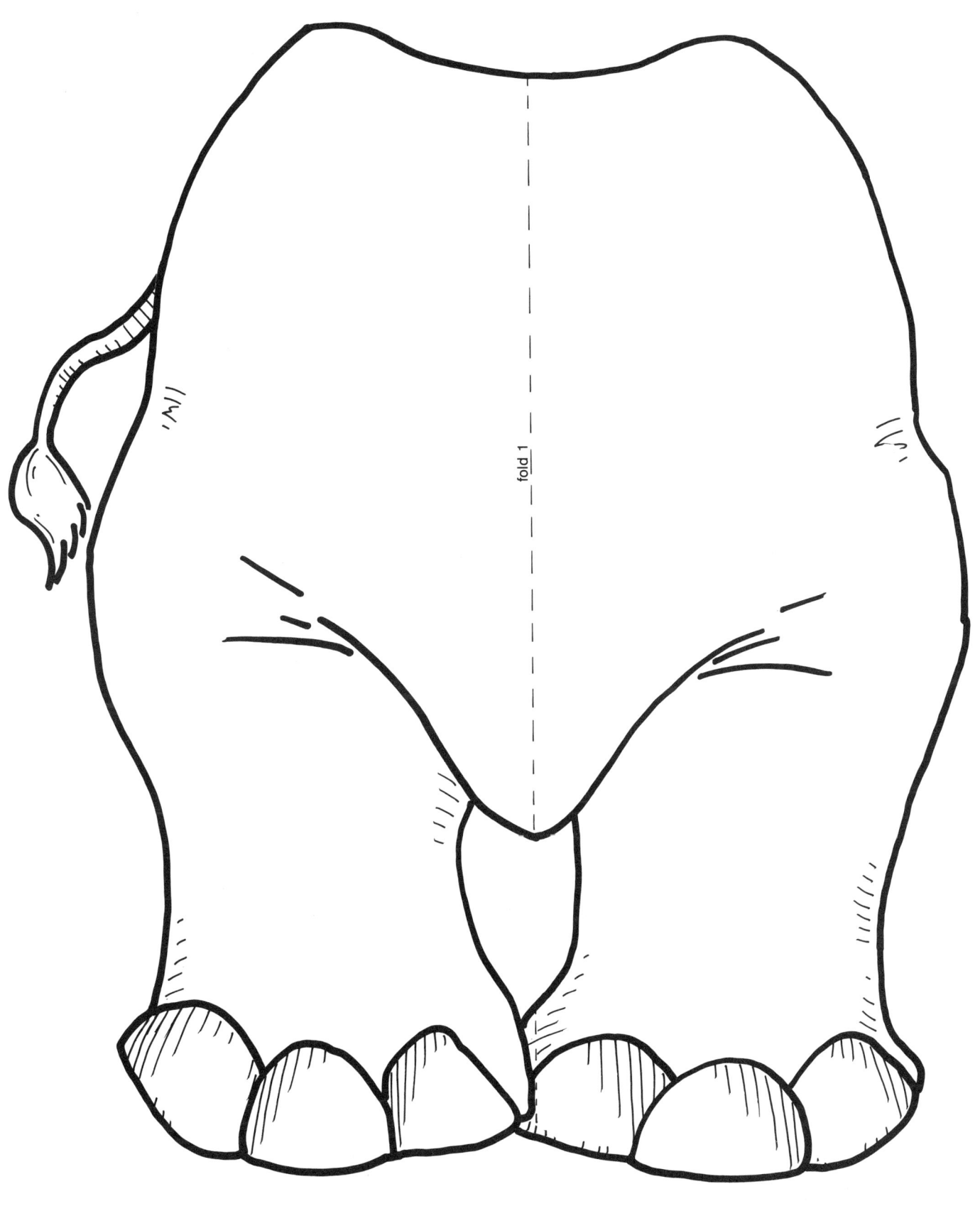

Apply glue only above fold 2 on the head.

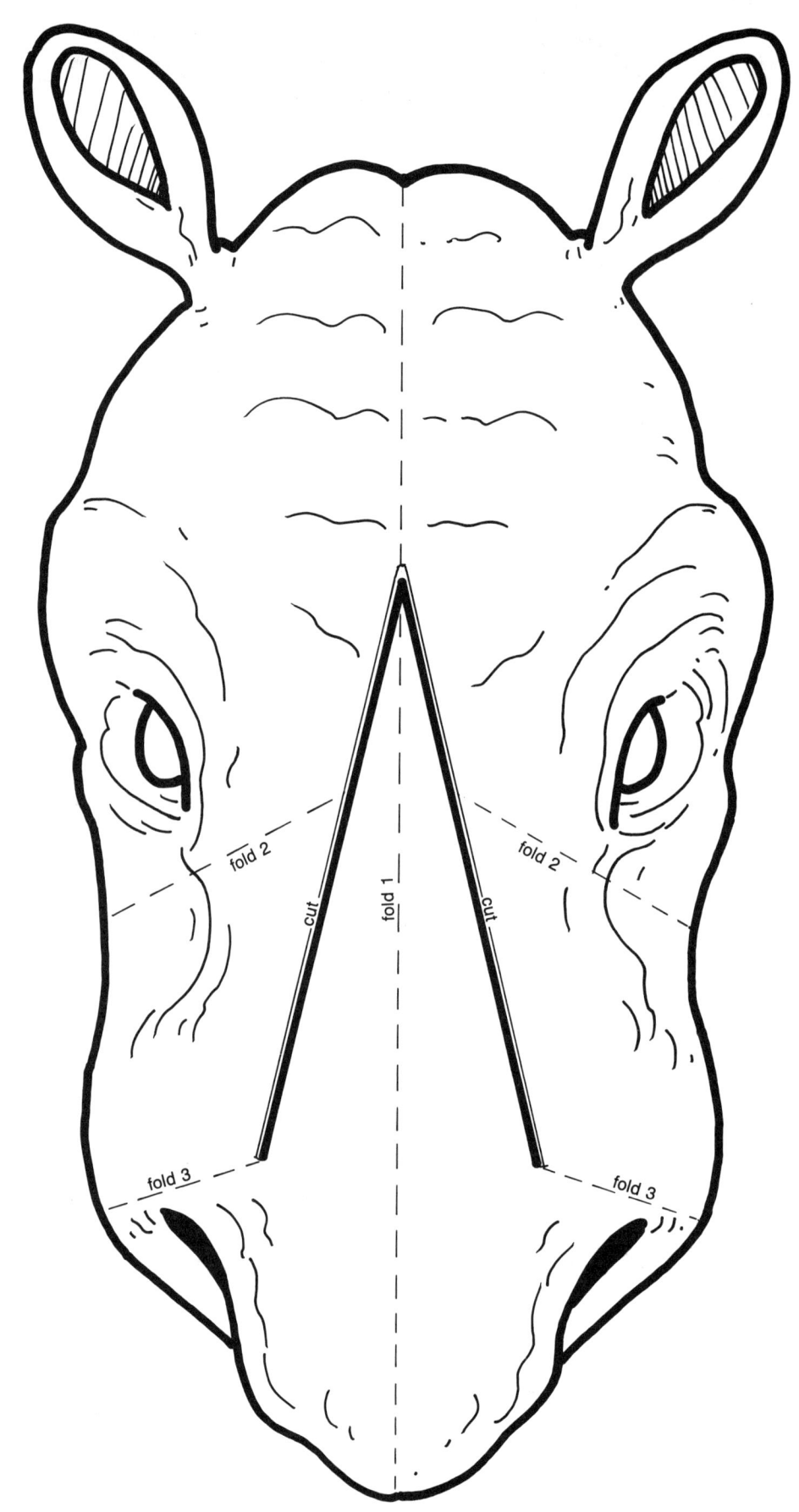